The Art of Hiring Leaders

A Guide for Nonprofit Organizations

Barbara J. Gilvar

A Note to Readers:

This book provides guidance as boards and search committees engage in searches and transition processes. It can help readers plan and proceed more knowledgeably. Its purpose is to raise awareness of the potential in a search and transition process, to describe the approach and methods a professional uses and to reduce the risks of searches which do not thoroughly assess their needs, do not look widely enough or do not carefully evaluate their choices.

Searches and transition processes are incredibly complex and involve many people within and outside the organization. This book cannot foresee every problem which could arise. Only the organization itself can ensure a successful transition through a thoughtful, thorough process. This book describes the key steps in that process and will help nonprofit boards recognize and avoid the most common mistakes. It is not a substitute for legal, financial or other professional advice.

Printed in the United States of America

Gilvar Publications

ISBN 0-9778233-1-8

The Art of Hiring Leaders:
A Guide for Nonprofit Organizations
Barbara J. Gilvar

To order: www.theartofhiringleaders.net
1 (800) 343-5540

Table of Contents

Preface

As an executive search consultant for more than two decades, I have been honored to work with dozens of dedicated groups in many fields: education, philanthropy, public broadcasting, the arts, community development, faith-based organizations, social services and health care. We shared a common goal — finding effective leadership to further the mission of an organization.

My work with organizations has been a continual learning process — both for me and for them. I shared my understanding with new employees in the firm where I was a partner and worked for nine years, providing orientation and on-going professional development. Then I taught search techniques to nonprofit groups which wanted to learn the art of recruiting well. Presenting workshops at conferences was another way of reaching board members and senior administrators who wanted to improve their hiring and recruiting including candidates from under-represented groups. A later development was training or "coaching" for individual organizations as a way to share information cost-effectively so that small nonprofits could knowledgeably carry out searches. This book is the product of that cumulative experience — conducting searches and teaching others how to conduct them.

In 1990, the National Association of Independent Schools asked me to create and edit *The Search Handbook* to improve the quality, outcome and long-term success of head-of-school searches. *The Art of Hiring Leaders* began with the desire to reach a broader audience so that other nonprofit organizations would have guidance in selecting executive directors. This new book incorporates insights gained since the publication of *The Search Handbook* and expands on themes which deserved more attention. This work also benefits from the feedback of committees who used the earlier book and from clients who reviewed this book.

Additional materials include more detailed guidance on creating effective search committees; suggestions on how to individualize aspects of the process depending on the organization's size, maturity and leadership history; a discussion of how leadership needs change over time; a chapter on leadership attributes and several chapters on strengthening the boards and the

V

organizations as they prepare for this major transition and the selection of the next executive director.

The major theme of *The Art of Hiring Leaders* is that a search is an opportunity; the goal of this book is to provide the information boards need to take maximum advantage of that opportunity. As I began my work with clients, most thought the search alone seemed like a daunting task — without even considering how to strengthen the organization at the same time. Boards that were initially nervous found that the methodology described in this book enabled them to successfully complete searches and they discovered that strengthening organizations was a natural result of a thoughtful search process.

A board chair who embraced the thoughtfulness of the process and who had worried about the prospects of hiring an "outsider", said at the conclusion of the search: "The biggest surprise was that there were so few surprises, because the search process pushed us to be clear about our goals and gave us such a thorough understanding of the person we chose." Another client who was worried about how the organization would do after he left, asked me to sit down with him and answer the many questions he had. At the end of our conversation he said: "Barbara, talking to you is so soothing." My hope is that the guidance this book offers will soothe anxieties by explaining a process which has been used successfully by many nonprofits and help a wide audience create successful search processes for their organizations.

May you find this book useful, enjoy your journey and be successful in your important work!

Barbara J. Gilvar

Boston, Massachusetts

Acknowledgments

I want to thank a long list of people who have contributed to this book in one way or another. If we start chronologically, Leah Mahan did the first reviews, made the first suggestions for where more detail was needed and encouraged me through what seemed interminable rewrites. John McMurtrie provided copy editing tips throughout the process. Johanna Wilson-White provided editing help; her suggestions and questions prompted me to reconsider what was included — and what was still needed. The result was new chapters and more detail in many phases. Elizabeth Schell patiently typed the early versions. Peter Kupfer provided copy editing of the expanded work. Janet Theurer and Tom Briggs of Theurer Briggs Design created the book and cover design. My thanks to each for your unique contributions.

Several former clients agreed to read chapters of interest to them or in their areas of expertise. Pat Williams, a lawyer, was especially helpful in reviewing the chapter on legal and ethical concerns. She also added perspective from her work as a board chair and member of two search committees, including one for an interim executive director. Doug Winkworth encouraged me to emphasize and expand on the opportunity possibilities. "Drive it home," as he said. I hope I did. He also provided insights from nineteen years as a board chair and member of two search committees. Doug Huff, a board member who had chaired a search committee, was most encouraging about the usefulness of the book. His exact words appear on the back cover. Mary Kay Eliot, a fund-raising consultant, reviewed my advice to the board about fund-raising. I wanted to be sure that what I believed matched her experience with organizations and their boards. Kay Edstene, former head of the Friends Council on Education, reviewed my Quakerly advice on decision-making to be sure I had worded it correctly. Deb Kost, who heads an organization, read the chapters on boards and remarked on how valuable it could be as they prepare for a search. My thanks for these perspectives which enrich the book.

Because I wanted the final chapter on leadership transitions to be as experience-based as the information on searches, I met with former clients and the people they chose to head their organizations to learn what their transitions could teach us. Transitions are a neglected topic and those fourteen interviews, with representatives of seven organizations, helped me illustrate more clearly the value of paying attention to the process of bringing a new leader into an organization and a community. My thanks to Rist Bonnefond, Dr. Mark Segar, Dick Roth, Jean Mooskin, Gary Smuckler, David Shapiro, Dr. Martha Bryans, Randy Lawlace, Dr. Kathy Schantz, Jim Hopkinson, Rose Hagan, Doug Cox, Doug Winkworth and Ken Seward.

Introduction

The purpose of this chapter is to describe the goals of the book, provide an overview of the search process and offer suggestions on how to use the book most effectively.

Shaping the results

A leadership transition is a critical event in a nonprofit organization, one which presents opportunities for growth and development — both for people and for the organization. One goal of this book is to help nonprofits recognize the potential in a search process and use this opportunity most productively.

Early questions and concerns

When the board of a nonprofit organization is facing a change in leadership it is naturally anxious about the responsibility, the process and the outcome. A board and its search committee will have questions immediately and other questions will emerge throughout the course of the search. The intent of this book is to answer the full range of questions.

Some of the first questions board members may have are:

- What is our role?
- What do we tell our constituents and when do we tell them?
- How do we find a great executive director?
- How do we explain our organization and its potential to people who do not know us?
- How long will the process take and how do we manage while the search is underway?
- What are the best ways to reduce anxiety during the search?
- Who should be on the search committee?
- With so much to do, why should we spend precious time planning?

When the board of a non-profit organization is facing a change in leadership it is naturally anxious about the responsibility, the process and the outcome.

In the next phase, some of the questions may be:

- What are the most effective ways to get the word out?
- Do we have to do more than just advertise?
- How do we learn to interpret resumes?
- What is the secret of interviewing well?
- Is it best to minimize our problems when talking with candidates?
- How can we be sure that references are telling us all we need to know?
- How do we support the success of our next executive director?
- What is the guarantee that our next leader will stay ten years or longer?

This book responds to process issues so that the search can run smoothly and people have confidence in it but as importantly the book examines strategic issues which can help to build stronger organizations as the search proceeds.

Those questions and many others are addressed in the following chapters. Some questions relate directly to the search process. This book responds to process issues so that the search can run smoothly and people have confidence in it but as importantly the book examines strategic issues which can help to build stronger organizations as the search proceeds.

The goals of the book

An overview of the goals:

- To help boards, and their appointed search committees, find the right leader for the organization's future success,
- To create a process which people trust and respect,
- To help people see how leadership transitions can be opportunities to invigorate and strengthen their organizations,
- To describe how to combine "big picture thinking", which provides a strong foundation for the search, with a step-by-step process that makes it all work,
- To support a successful search by providing a common base of information so that each search committee or board member is a knowledgeable participant and continues to learn throughout the process,
- To help boards and search committees use their knowledge to make good decisions for their organizations, and
- To encourage a thoughtful transition process to support the success of the new executive director.

The intended audience

Any nonprofit organization which uses a search committee in the process of hiring an executive director can benefit from the material contained in this book. The breadth of information will provide an overview of topics critical to the success of the search and the transition, including strategic thinking about board development and organizational goals. To complement the overview there are detailed steps to provide a search committee with the information it needs to knowledgably conduct each phase of the search.

The level of detail can guide board or search committee members who are beginning their first search process. It can also guide those who were not satisfied with the process or the results of an earlier search. Organizations that cannot afford to hire a consultant can use the book to develop an over-all plan, carry out each phase of the search knowledgably and learn to make informed decisions throughout the process.

The methodology described in this book has supported the work of many search committees in fields as varied as education, the environment, social services, human services, the arts and philanthropy. Some of the organizations were faith-based; this methodology could be used by search committees entrusted with the task of selecting pastoral leaders.

Although nonprofits differ in size, maturity and purpose, the steps described in this book can be tailored to fit individual organizations. Some of the topics are universally applicable.

- Each organization can create search materials uniquely its own which describe mission, history, programs, goals and the leadership it is seeking,
- Each organization can learn to identify its board and leadership needs and to reach a new stage of development in the process, and
- The information on networking, evaluating applications, interviewing and conducting references is applicable to any nonprofit.

While nonprofits differ in some characteristics, they have some things in common — each is supported by a board of directors and by a leader/executive director. This book includes several chapters on boards and leadership, critical components of a successful search. Chapter Three explains how boards develop, the natural growth processes and ways to strengthen the

The level of detail can guide board or search committee members who are beginning their first search process. It can also guide those who were not satisfied with the process or the results of an earlier search.

effectiveness of any board, at any stage, during the search process. Chapter Five describes the significant ways that leadership needs change as an organization grows and develops, information which would help a search committee assess its current leadership priorities.

The intent of *The Art of Hiring Leaders* is to provide more information than the earlier book, *The Search Handbook*; this book encourages strategic thinking, board building and search planning to strengthen the search process and transition. *The Art of Hiring Leaders* is designed so that a non-profit organization has the information to work on board and organizational development and to conduct a successful search process without outside help. Many search committees who used the earlier book chose to also work with a consultant. If an organization wants to consider using a consultant there is information on consultants in Appendix C.

Overview and commonly used terms

The following section is an introduction to the terms used throughout the book. It also provides an overview of the process.

The board of directors has the ultimate responsibility and authority for hiring the executive director. It is key to the success of the entire process, providing leadership in creating the vision, planning the search process, appointing a search committee, selecting a new leader, making the transition to new leadership and providing guidance and support to the executive director. The term "trustee" is used interchangeably with the term "board member."

The executive director, or head of the organization, reports to the board of directors and carries out its policies.

For some organizations, an **interim or acting director** may provide leadership while the search for a permanent director is underway.

Constituents are the administrators, staff, clients, board members, funders — everyone affiliated with the organization in some way.

Search refers to the executive search process — the hiring of leaders through a pro-active process which begins by defining the organization's strengths and challenges, continues by identifying and evaluating candidates and concludes with an informed selection and a plan for the new leader's transition.

Boards appoint **search committees** to have representation and wisdom in this important work. Members of the committee represent the nonprofit's constituencies. This committee has many responsibilities, from developing a job description to recommending finalists to the board.

A **written description of the organization**, including the role of the executive director, is produced by the search committee with input from the community. It is unique to each organization, a comprehensive document that describes the organization's history, mission, strengths and challenges and, within that context, the specific criteria for the next leader.

The outreach phase is next in the search process and begins with a comprehensive plan for advertising, contacting sources and actively recruiting people who meet the criteria.

Potential candidates are people whom a search committee hopes will apply, people it is trying to recruit or interest in the job.

Applicants, or **candidates**, are people who send letters and résumés to apply for the position.

Evaluating applications is the responsibility of the search committee using the criteria developed with community input and written into the job description. The purpose of the evaluation is to select people to interview, those whom the committee judges to be the best matches.

Semi-finalists are candidates initially interviewed by the search committee. Because of confidentiality, the committee alone evaluates applications and conducts these first interviews.

The finalists are the candidates the committee recommends to the board, those people who seem to be the best fit. At this time, the candidacies of the finalists are public and they meet with all of the organization's constituencies.

References are the people whom the search committee and board will contact to discuss a candidate's experience and qualifications.

Written references are additional materials, which candidates may provide, but they are not a substitute for talking with people who know the candidates well.

The selection process is the board's responsibility. It uses all of the information gathered during the search process to select the next executive director from the finalists recommended by the search committee.

A transition process, after the selection of the new executive director, confirms priorities and goals with the new leader and helps him or her enter the community thoughtfully and knowledgeably.

How to use the book

The explanation of terms is a brief introduction to a complex subject. Each of these terms will have more meaning as the process unfolds; each has at least one chapter devoted to it. The chapters are intentionally short so that board and search committee members can easily find discussions of specific topics as they need them. A good approach to using this book is to skim the entire contents to get an overview of the process, and then to re-read specific chapters when they are relevant. Topics are cross-referenced so that a reader can find more detailed information, as needed, or understand the importance of a particular phase of the search to the overall success of the process. The Checklist at the end of the book is another way to remember the important pieces at each stage of the process.

This chapter explained the goals of the book and defined frequently used terms; it also provided an overview of the process. The next chapter is devoted to explaining the role of the board as the transition begins.

The Board's Role in the Transition

The purpose of this chapter is to describe the special opportunities and responsibilities which the board has in this period of leadership transition.

Introduction

Looking at this chapter, the board's first question might be "Why are we focusing on the board when we are anxious to start the search?" A search for an executive director is an opportunity for the board to have a significant, long-term impact on the organization, and this discussion and the following chapters will help ensure that the board is ready to take advantage of that opportunity.

This period of board leadership has the potential to be a time of real growth in the board's understanding of its leadership role and the ways it can guide the organization. The board has the opportunity to create the "big picture" for the organization and link the vision directly to short and long-term goals and the hiring of the next executive director. Ideally, the opportunity to positively influence the future will motivate board members to participate actively because they understand the importance of their role and that this is the time when they can really make a difference. All of the decisions about the search process will flow from the board's work — from their initial communication to the community to the selection of the search committee, the choice of the next executive director and the completion of the transition process. Over the years, it has become more and more obvious that the effectiveness of boards is a determining factor in successful searches.

One of my wise former clients observed that the search for a new leader "is one of those rare times when the board is called upon to be most truly board-like." A board chair for nineteen years who served on two search committees for heads of organizations, he stressed the importance of the board's role when he stated that "A search is truly about the board being a success."

This chapter will raise topics which trustees might not think of early in the search process because of the number of items which need their attention or

A search for an executive director is an opportunity for the board to have a significant, long-term impact on the organization, and this discussion and the following chapters will help ensure that the board is ready to take advantage of that opportunity.

because the concept of search is new to them. The goal is for the board, its executive director and the organization to be successful in the long-term. That success depends on the foundation the board establishes at the beginning of the search process as it proactively defines a vision, evaluates its own development needs and plans the search process. This opportunity for creating a vision and enabling the board's development can easily be missed because the board is distracted by the range of tasks it faces or is listening to those who believe that just moving ahead will solve everything. Reflection and planning will reveal how complex "everything" can be and how easily the board can provide true leadership and positively influence the future of the organization.

The board's public role at the beginning of the search

A search for an executive director represents a major change and the result is that each constituency will have concerns. As the board prepares a time and place for working on vision, it also needs to attend to the community's anxiety at the beginning of this transition; the public role is to provide continuity and re-assurance. The most immediate task is to convey confidence that the organization is stable and ready to move forward. News of the change in leadership can be less jarring when people are assured that transitions are part of an organization's natural development and can be opportunities for moving forward in new ways.

The board can also help to ease the transition in the following ways:

- Being visible. Because the board provides continuity, its presence is important during a transition. Ideally, the board is known to the community so its presence will not seem like a response to a crisis, but a bridge to the future.

- Being calm, thoughtful and deliberate. Developing a vision process so the organization realizes the full advantages of this opportunity. Creating a clear plan for moving ahead so the community will have confidence in the process. Assuring, and then demonstrating, that the process will be inclusive and comprehensive.

- Helping others see a change of leadership as part of the continuing development of an organization. Reminding people of the organization's accomplishments and hurdles it has already overcome puts this transition in perspective. With that focus, the transition will no longer seem like a crisis, but an opportunity to come together around a common vision for the future.

- Communicating the search plan widely and effectively to keep the broader community informed about the search process. Because well-conducted searches take months, providing effective communication will require frequent updates through personal contact, letters, newsletters and the organization's Web site. While the search committee and board understand the progress of the search, others do not. In a vacuum there will be anxiety and anxiety produces rumors. The facts are better.

The board's strategic role

The board's strategic role is to lead the thinking about the potential of the organization as a foundation for its search for a new executive director. The vision is the basis for knowing what to look for in new leadership. Searches and transitions can offer an important opportunity for organizations to accomplish what they already know they want to do but have not yet had a chance to accomplish. For other organizations, there might not have been the opportunity to think collectively about the future. Whether a board is reaffirming a vision or creating a new one, the work offers the opportunity for the board to come together around a vision in preparation for the search. A board session devoted to talking about vision can be the first step in making the vision a reality.

The vision is the basis for knowing what to look for in new leadership.

Vision building or strategic planning will ensure that the next executive director is someone who fits the organization's defined needs. After the board is clear about its vision/future goals, it can use the following questions to concretely link its vision with the search:

- Which of our strengths will help us the most in achieving our future goals?
- Where do we need to become stronger to achieve our goals?
- What characteristics and experiences of candidates relate directly to these goals?

Given the amount of time and energy the search process will require, the board's objective is to begin the work of defining vision and understand how it links to the search for the next executive director. Developing a more formal strategic plan and implementation steps can come later.

As the board creates and nourishes a vision and links it to the search for a new executive director, it is making the most of a significant opportunity for the organization and demonstrating the leadership the community needs. Because of this work, the board will be better prepared to guide and communicate with its search committee, with the community and ultimately with candidates.

The work on vision and strategic thinking is separate from the board's development of a search plan, which is the subject of Chapter Four. That plan works on the details of having an effective search process and provides further guidance for the search committee's work.

There are many and varied tasks ahead which will benefit from the active participation and leadership of each board member, an opportunity for board building and identifying new strengths among trustees. It can also be a fulfilling time as the board realizes the importance of its leadership to the organization's development. Another benefit of having an active and knowledgeable board is that it will be attractive to candidates the organization would like to attract.

Actions needed now and those which can wait

At the start of the search process the board must determine which priorities need immediate attention and which will be strengthened by waiting until a new leader is hired. If there is an urgency, such as the need to find new space, obviously that cannot wait for the conclusion of the search. If the organization has gathered momentum for a strategic planning process, it may need to continue so that it will not lose momentum and further disrupt the community. Or, the vision-building the board and community will engage in can use those energies to support the search process, and the strategic planning can occur later when it can include the new leader.

Each organization has to assess its particular needs and the board's task is to find the right balance between short-term priorities and longer-term goals. The decision will be influenced by the size of the nonprofit and the people resources available because people are engaged in the vision work, the planning work and the search.

A difficult personnel issue is one area where an out-going executive director may prefer to delay a decision. It is usually to the advantage of the search process and the next executive director to follow through on such a decision when it is apparent that it is necessary. A thoughtful plan by the current executive director, with the support of the board, can determine the best way to proceed. A major consideration is the impact of delaying any decision until the new leader begins. Natural questions are "What is lost by having someone stay when it is obvious that he or she should go?" and "How will having to let someone go soon after arriving affect the initial perceptions of the new executive director?"

Identifying organizational issues

The board will begin the search process by defining its vision and the community will add its insights later in the process, (discussed further in Chapter Eleven). Hearing the perspectives of all constituencies is an important part of the board's learning process, the foundation for launching a search which is based on aspirations and self-knowledge.

The insights provided by constituents can confirm the board's vision and possibly add new dimensions. The constituent meetings may also raise issues, some of which the trustees may have already identified and others that may be new to them. These problems may be small and easily remedied, or they may be significant. Many issues, given more attention or added resources -- either people or financial — can be addressed during the search process. Left unsolved, problems can have a negative effect on the search. It may be tempting for a board to assume that the new leader can fix everything, but good candidates may be wary of an organization that is waiting for deliverance.

It may be tempting for a board to assume that the new leader can fix everything, but good candidates may be wary of an organization that is waiting for deliverance.

Beginning to solve problems now will have a positive effect on the organization and the attractiveness of the position; the following scenario illustrates one success story. A committee engaged in a search to replace a long-term leader was surprised and embarrassed to discover that the organization's reputation had seriously declined. It communicated this unhappy news to the board, which struggled to find a way to respond appropriately and move forward with the search. The board began to address the problems and make policies that would strengthen the organization. As a result, the board became more knowledgeable and effective and, because of its progress, was able to hire an excellent executive director who continued the positive momentum.

Fund-raising

In recent years, executive directors are spending more of their time raising money. The emphasis will vary with different organizations, but has to become part of developing the goals and be balanced with other priorities. In large nonprofits, development staff can support the executive directors and the boards. For smaller nonprofits, it is the executives and the boards who provide the fund-raising leadership. For those smaller organizations, boards need to play a stronger role in fund-raising during the search period and through the early stages of a new leader's tenure.

Many boards, which are not very experienced in fund-raising or have not been very successful at it, are hopeful that new leaders will make an immediate difference. Raising money is something every nonprofit leader has to be prepared to do — with the assistance and leadership of the board. However, a new executive director needs time to learn about the organization in order to become a strong and well-informed advocate who can speak eloquently and effectively about the organization and its needs. The transition strategy, described in Chapter Twenty One, will include many opportunities to showcase the organization and its new leader so that a well-planned transition can be building the foundation for future fund-raising. For the immediate future, however, this responsibility belongs to the board.

Strong candidates will assess the strength of the board and its willingness to play a role in fund-raising so building this capacity is important for the search.

If the trustees are already active in the development efforts, they can continue this work seamlessly. If the board has not been active in development efforts in the past, this point of transition is the time to begin preparing for active participation. Associations offer fund-raising sessions at their conferences and many have staff who will provide workshops for individual boards. Most associations can also identify similar organizations which recently learned to fund-raise successfully; one of those board members may be willing to share ideas. Or, a workshop by a fund-raising consultant is a way to get to know someone who may be of help at a later stage as well. Most boards find that someone who is not a board member can be more effective in "jump-starting" the board's transition to a "culture" of fund-raising. Strong candidates will assess the strength of the board and its willingness to play a role in fund-raising so building this capacity is important for the search.

If an organization is in the middle of a capital campaign, when the executive director announces he or she is leaving, it will probably continue the campaign — but with stronger board leadership. Usually a nonprofit that knows its leader is leaving will postpone a major capital campaign because the uncertainty will diminish the chances of success and so many people resources will be absorbed by the search.

There are at least two possible exceptions to the need for postponing a campaign. A retiring or departing leader may want to lead the fund-raising effort in the "silent phase", when requests are made to major donors, because he or she knows that people are likely to honor him or her in this way. The second exception is when a board expected to lead the effort, has the connections and commitment to proceeding, and therefore believes the campaign will succeed.

Without a beloved and willing executive director or an active, connected and committed board, the best alternative is to begin planning but delay the start of the actual campaign. The clarity around goals which develops through the search process and the enthusiasm for the new leader can result in a more successful capital campaign, slightly delayed. In the meantime, the board can increase its skills and comfort in this area.

Finances

Nervousness about finances often makes boards hope the new leader will solve the organization's financial problems; however this presents several obstacles to the search and transition. Potential candidates will be reluctant to join an organization whose finances are shaky and whose only plan is to have the new executive director fix the problem. If the board cannot solve the financial issues immediately it can develop a plan and some initial actions which will help to reassure candidates, staff and donors.

Potential candidates will be reluctant to join an organization whose finances are shaky and whose only plan is to have the new executive director fix the problem.

A board which is working effectively on fund-raising or finance is strengthening the organization and the chances of finding candidates whose skills and vision will help meet all of its goals. Those goals surely will include program areas. An over-emphasis on finances or fund-raising, rather than on mission and program, may limit the number of talented candidates who decide to apply. Candidates understand the need for resource development but also want to be connected with the programs and staff.

Some of these suggestions about fund-raising or financial issues will mean greater emphasis on the board's responsibilities and growth, an important factor in recruiting strong candidates. Overall, as a board develops its capabilities it will be better prepared to hire, guide and support the next executive director.

The decision-making process for the selection of the executive director

While the final selection of the new leader is months away, this is also the time to be specific about who makes that decision. The board of trustees is responsible for hiring an executive director which is usually clearly stated in the bylaws. This fact needs to be clearly communicated to the search committee and the community along with the following explanation. The board appoints a search committee to do a great deal of important work and will depend on the committee's wisdom in identifying and presenting a number of finalists for the board's consideration. Having the responsibility of selecting the next executive director from among unranked finalists allows the board to fulfill its responsibility. They will also "own" the decision, an important factor in their ongoing work with the next executive director. See Chapter Seventeen which discusses the selection process in more depth.

A former client expressed her feelings this way: "The Saturday meeting was wonderful. I really enjoyed watching us come around to a heartfelt consensus. I hope all boards are able to 'own their decision.'"

It is important for the board to develop agreement and clarity about the decision-making process in this planning phase, one more step in the board's recognition of its leadership role in this process. The next step is to be clear in communicating with the search committee and with the community – at the beginning of the search before there are any misunderstandings. In some communities, particularly where there has not been a search for many years, this board announcement may not be comfortable because the community will feel that it is being left out. In its first communication with the community the board would explain the inclusiveness of the search process through the composition of the search committee, the opportunity for the community to share their insights at the beginning of the process, the value of those insights, the plan for communicating throughout the search process and how the community will be involved when the finalists visit. This explanation of community involvement in the search process can be reassuring and it de-mystifies the process.

Each board can assume that the community is likely to be anxious because of the leadership change. The longer the anxiety continues, the more likely it is that politics will become an issue. Thoughtful planning and good communication will lessen anxiety and politicking.

At the start of the search process, the board will want to stress its require-ment for a number of qualified and viable finalists to ensure that the resulting recommendations from the search committee will offer the board true choices. Conversations and/or informal reports to the board in the course of the search are opportunities to keep the board meaningfully engaged. The section in Chapter Thirteen "Knowing when the networking is done" is a guide for the search committee and can be the basis of a useful dialogue with the board. Additional perspectives and questions always help, and the decision about when to end the networking is a critical one in the search process.

When the search committee knows its responsibilities and authority from the beginning, it is more comfortable with a leadership role in the search process and a supporting role as the board makes its decision. If the deci-sion-making authority is not clear at the start of the process, people can have a different sense about who makes the decision, and unraveling the problem later tends to reflect negatively on the process.

If the decision-making authority is not clear at the start of the process, people can have a different sense about who makes the deci-sion, and unraveling the problem later tends to reflect negatively on the process.

Another practical reason for the search committee to offer multiple, unranked finalists to the board is that a candidate may withdraw at the last moment. The reasons could be a belated change of mind, a counter-offer from his or her current employer, a more attractive offer from another group or family issues and objections. The good news is that when the search is done well, the finalists are all qualified and viable can-didates. One search committee member, whose organization lost its "first" choice, said three months later: "What possessed us not to recog-nize that the person who accepted was the best choice all along?" Having a finalist withdraw, and having to select another candidate, occurs often enough to confirm the wisdom of presenting multiple strong and viable finalists to the board.

This chapter has begun to prepare the board for its role in a successful search. The following chapter deals with strate-gies for board development which can be incorporated into its work during the search process.

Strengthening Boards

The purpose of this chapter is to explain how boards change as nonprofit organizations mature and evolve and to offer strategies for building board capabilities.

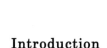

Introduction

The simple objective of this chapter is to prompt board members to ask: "Where do we need to develop in order to be ready for this search and the selection and support of the next executive director?"

One of the most important duties which boards have is to select, support and evaluate the executive director. While many books focus on board effectiveness as their primary topic, this chapter and the following observations are specifically designed to prepare boards for their role during leadership transitions. The simple objective of this chapter is to prompt board members to ask: "Where do we need to develop in order to be ready for this search and the selection and support of the next executive director?" Boards will be better prepared for their important leadership roles if they identify their professional development needs and make growth work part of their work on the transition process.

Boards change each time they select new executive directors. One important and immediate difference is that boards are called upon to provide much more guidance because they carry the organizations' history, values, traditions and visions for the future. Ideally, each board will find useful ideas in this chapter to support its evolving role.

The age of an organization influences the way its board functions and the way that a board's role is changing over time. Boards go through stages of development just as the organizations they serve grow and change. The difference is that boards usually are not anticipating how the changes will affect them. The following description of the stages of board development provides a foundation for a board to recognize how the nonprofit has changed and what those changes mean for the board. Understanding what to expect can make it easier for a board to see how its role is changing and to begin planning how to evolve to the next level. This board work will prepare it to attract talented leadership and form a strong partnership with the new executive director.

The strategies for growth and professional development are useful for every stage of maturity and development. The few minutes required to read this chapter can help boards adjust their practices or move in new directions. This discussion of professional development may simply highlight areas that boards intended to work on next, areas that can now be incorporated into the transition work.

Younger organizations

The boards of younger nonprofits function differently than those of more mature organizations. New boards are often composed of hands-on volunteers because there are few paid staff. The initial informality and blurring of staff and board roles is common. As organizations mature and gain more staff, some of the hands-on work the boards did is no longer as necessary. For board members, this can result in a difficult and awkward transition period.

As nonprofits grow, they take on different organizational structures to accommodate new goals, program expansion and added staff. At this point there is more definition of individual roles and perhaps the first organizational chart. The addition of professional staff means that they are able to manage all aspects of the operations without relying on board volunteers.[1]

As organizations mature and develop through new programs and staff, most will discuss how these changes will affect them. The role of their boards also matures and develops, but because this evolution is less clear it usually receives less focused attention.

As boards continue to move away from day-to-day involvement and to understand their evolving role in policy-making, the changes require an adjustment of roles — which is rarely easy. This is the time when trustees, whose hands-on services were needed in the past, are learning to resist filling, or second-guessing, the roles of new staff. At the same time, the maturing organizations are developing more formality and structure in board/staff communication. Hard-working trustees may feel at somewhat of a loss now, uncertain about how to define their new roles.

The good news is that boards have the opportunity to evolve to a new, different and potentially equally satisfying role. With more staff, boards have the opportunity to concentrate on vision, fiscal health, hiring, supporting and

The strategies for growth and professional development are useful for every stage of maturity and development. The few minutes required to read this chapter can help boards adjust their practices or move in new directions.

[1] For some organizations volunteers, including board members who work in program areas, are an important part of the mission. This should not affect the evolution to a policy-making board.

A board's understanding of its role is particularly important as candidates assess what their relationship with the board is likely to be and whether the board understands and will respect the appropriate boundaries.

evaluating the executive director, assuring that the mission is being fulfilled and that there are long-range strategies in place. Organizations can become stronger when the board and staff balance each other and have expertise in their respective roles. A board's understanding of its role is particularly important as candidates assess what their relationship with the board is likely to be and whether the board understands and will respect the appropriate boundaries.

Policies and operations

As organizations go through this transition, it is useful to have reminders of the complementary roles of boards as policy-makers and staff as those who implement those policies. Open and good-natured questions are one strategy for discussing where responsibilities lie. Boards and their executive directors can recognize the boundaries and the "gray" areas by raising questions. For example: "Is this a policy issue or an operational issue, or does it overlap?" Or, either party could begin a discussion with an acknowledgment or reminder about roles. Executive directors could say: "I know this is an operational issue, but I wanted to let you know or ask your advice." In another situation, board chairs could say: "This is clearly a policy issue, but we want the benefit of your expertise."

The phrasing of the questions is a request for advice as well as a reminder of the complementary roles and the boundaries — and a useful strategy for all boards. Seeking advice is also a good use of talent; avoiding discussions of "gray" areas could result in losing valuable perspectives.

More mature organizations

If term limits do not exist, boards may want to initiate staggered terms to provide continuity and to make room for new trustees.

As nonprofits grow and develop new goals, the composition of their boards begins to change to keep up with the organizations' growth. New goals or requirements of funders may mean that boards need to seek additional skills and abilities in new members. This is usually the time that boards begin to look beyond their circle of friends and acquaintances for future trustees. As organizations mature, they expect more help in fund-raising from their boards, which also begins to alter the composition of membership. If term limits do not exist, boards may want to initiate staggered terms to provide continuity and to make room for new trustees.

Bringing in new trustees, and recognizing the need for different skills, is a major shift which requires focused attention and dialogues about why the changes are necessary and what the potential benefits are. Managing this transition thoughtfully can result in stronger boards. The challenge is to welcome new members while valuing the dedication to mission and the strengths of existing boards.

In some cases, a board will be working with an executive director who has served for a longer time than any trustee. In that case, the board is usually more responsive than proactive. This requires the board to shift to a more appropriately active role so that it can accurately define its goals and prepare itself for its leadership role when the new executive director is in place. After the long-term tenures of strong executive directors, boards have to candidly evaluate their readiness to move forward as strong and independent boards, how much time and attention is required and whether the "board building" and changing of board "culture" needs outside assistance to ease the process.

Strong, successful, long-term leaders can also affect the search by becoming the model for the next executive director. There are several dangers in this. The first is that the organization and the external environment have changed. New goals will translate into the need for different skills or a different emphasis on them.

The second danger is the assumption that the organization needs another strong leader, similar in leadership style. It is easy to overlook how many years of building relationships, rapport and good will went into the outgoing director's ability to be a decisive leader. A new leader will not have that history, and moving too quickly or making precipitous changes can cause people in the organization to resist any leadership efforts.

Boards need to be aware of the dangers of not analyzing how their organizations have changed and not analyzing the qualities of leadership a new executive director will need to succeed. Developing a clear understanding of history is the basis for defining what is needed at the present time. This analysis will help boards in hiring, conducting references and becoming knowledgeable advisors to the new executive directors – not simply their admirers. Because a board provides the continuity and a deep knowledge of the organization, their role is to guide the new leader.

This analysis will help boards in hiring, conducting references and becoming knowledgeable advisors to the new executive directors – not simply their admirers.

Developing an effective board

Whatever their stage of development, boards and organizations have created patterns of work and relationships which are now part of the organizations' culture. Often there are "influential" trustees and "others". That division may limit the development of the full boards and perhaps even the leadership abilities of the executive directors. In well-functioning groups each person is contributing and therefore has a valuable role. Developing effective boards, rather than having a group of individual trustees, is a continuing process.

This time of transition is a natural moment for boards to reflect on their work and how effectively they use the skills of all their members. A board's work in creating a vision as a foundation for its searches, described in Chapter Two, is a good beginning for engaging all members of the board. Committees on trustees can continue the focus on the development of each person, which will strengthen the work of the whole board. During the search process, boards and organizations will need and benefit from having trustees who are thoroughly engaged and effective.

Looking ahead to working with new a executive director is a natural time for boards to plan their future because they must be ready to support the searches, the transitions to new leadership and the new leaders.

At every level of maturity, most boards struggle with having the commitment of all members, with clarity about their goals, roles and responsibilities, and how to be most effective for the organization. Looking ahead to working with new a executive director is a natural time for boards to plan their future because they must be ready to support the searches, the transitions to new leadership and the new leaders.

Once boards have completed their visioning, developed their search plans and created search committees they have accomplished a great deal. Ideally, that sense of purpose and accomplishment will inspire boards to continue their development. With major pieces of the search in place, boards can turn their attention to further growth so they are fully able to support the ongoing transition work. The preliminary work of preparing for the searches may well have identified areas where boards realize they need to develop further. The committees on trustees can now build on the boards' accomplishments and suggest ways to build the boards' capacity for continuing, high-level support.

Organizations may find they need assistance in moving to new levels and different roles. Some associations offer technical assistance or can recommend places to find it. The most useful professional development plans are tailored to a board's specific needs rather than applying a pre-packaged product. When a board is clear about what it needs, it can be specific about finding support in the areas that are important to it. If a board chooses to hire an organizational development consultant, talking with other organizations referred by the consultant will help ensure that the match is a good one. The chapter on references and the appendix information on checking the references of search consultants contain useful information.

The more a board has developed as an effective and cohesive unit, the more attractive the executive director position will be to candidates. Unorganized or divisive boards will diminish a nonprofit's ability to attract "star" talent.

Developing an evaluation process

This time of transition is the opportunity to define goals and evaluation processes to shape the future — and the organizations' progress in getting there. Some boards set annual goals and evaluate themselves and the executive directors. Some do one but not the other. If some part of the evaluation process is underdeveloped, changing that can become a priority now. The single most important thing that boards can do for their organizations and to support the success of the executive directors is to establish clear goals and an effective way to evaluate the effectiveness of the work of the boards and the executive directors in meeting those goals.

Chapter Twenty One describes how to create mutual goals and an evaluation process to help boards and their executive directors become more focused and effective. Starting to think about evaluation processes now will prepare the boards to discuss the topic with potential candidates, who are likely to ask about it.

The single most important thing that boards can do for their organizations and to support the success of the executive directors is to establish clear goals and an effective way to evaluate the effectiveness of the work of the boards and the executive directors in meeting those goals.

This chapter described how the role of boards changes and develops along with the growth of their organizations. The next chapter describes the work of planning the search for a new executive director.

Planning a Leadership Search

The purpose of this chapter is to help boards set the foundation for a successful search process by identifying the major elements to consider.

Introduction

A change in leadership is unsettling and it can feel like a long and important journey without directions. Planning provides a map. Although there is much to do at the start of a search and an anxiety to get started, it is better to resist the temptation to rush into it because most boards are not certain what "it" is.

The search will go more smoothly and be more successful when all the tasks are identified and discussed in advance. Planning enables a board to be proactive in preparing for success because it knows what can make the search successful and how to avoid the most common problems.

No matter why the current executive director is leaving, people will be anxious and have a range of emotions — from sadness to relief. There will be uncertainty about the best way to proceed with the search process and, at the same time, there will be a desire to move ahead quickly to restore a sense of stability. The board feels the weight of responsibility. It may never have been through a search process before, or it may have been through them too often. Staff are anxious about how the organization will change. Funders are concerned about programs and continuity. The board will be better prepared to respond to these multiple concerns when it has identified the issues and developed its plan.

The benefits of planning

A few hours of planning can have a positive influence on the entire search process. The time spent at the beginning of the process has benefits for each critical decision and on every phase of the search. The positive results can include:

- setting a tone for the process and instilling confidence in it,

- reducing anxiety,

- encouraging community building and the creation of a shared vision,

- creating clear criteria, before there are candidates, to provide a framework for the process and avoid decisions based on personalities or single issues,

- helping to identify the tasks, the potential problems, the people who could be involved in leadership roles, and

- making the entire process more effective, efficient and successful.

The hours spent planning will help the board communicate clearly with all constituencies; the result will be reduced anxiety. The process of thinking through what needs to be done will probably ease the board's anxiety as well. This should offset any pressure to fill the leadership vacuum hastily, which is usually a mistake; the chances are high that rushing the selection could result in an unsuccessful appointment. In the end, that failure would become much more time-consuming, expensive and anxiety-provoking for the organization.

The hours spent planning will help the board communicate clearly with all constituencies; the result will be reduced anxiety. The process of thinking through what needs to be done will probably ease the board's anxiety as well.

Initial planning considerations

These are the elements of a plan which will help a board get a solid start:

- Determine the values which will guide the search (discussed below and in Chapter Seven),

- Create a vision from the board's perspective (discussed in this chapter and in Chapter Two),

- Identify problems which the board must work on (Chapter Two),

- Project a desired timeline (see search timeline below),

- Plan the initial communication to the community (discussed in this chapter and in Chapter Eight),

- Discuss how the community will be meaningfully involved (introduced here and developed further in Chapter Eleven),

- Appoint the chair of the search committee and state the role and responsibilities of the committee (discussed in Chapter Two),

- Care for the outgoing executive director (discussed under "Lengthy notice and retirements" in this chapter and in Chapter Twenty One),

- Determine if interim leadership is necessary (discussed in this chapter, under "Timeframe and preparation for it," and in Appendix B),
- Investigate the salaries of executive directors at comparable organizations to develop a salary range (Chapter Fifteen), and
- Decide on a budget for the search (discussed in "Budget matters" in this chapter).

This chapter covers several topics which only appear here. Examples are the search timeline and establishing a budget for the search. Some topics are introduced here and also discussed in depth in other chapters. While values, vision and communication appear in other places as well, they are emphasized here because of their importance in providing a foundation for the search.

Values and the search

It is worth the board's time to state the values it wants to guide the search process.

Nonprofit organizations have values which guide their work. Those values have meaning for the search process as well, but the connection may not be immediately obvious. It is worth the board's time to state the values it wants to guide the search process. Some of these may be re-statements of policies which already exist — an example is a policy about inclusion and diversity.

Other values will have meaning for the search but may not yet be explicit. Some examples are to maintain confidentiality, as appropriate, during the search process and to ask each candidate the same set of questions, so the interviews are equitable. Chapter Seven, "Legal and Ethical Considerations," can help a board develop other value statements specifically for the search. A logical question would be: "Why not just use someone else's list?" Creating a statement of values is a useful board exercise because identifying them gives them more meaning.

As members of the search committee discuss how the value statements affect the search process, the values gain more meaning and provide an important basis for their work.

The statements the board develops will reaffirm the values people may not talk about very often. Once written down they will be useful guidelines for the search committee, a place to return for guidance on issues which may not be predictable at the start of a search. As members of the search committee discuss how the value statements affect the search process, the values gain more meaning and provide an important basis for their work. Without these very direct statements there is the danger that members of search committees will make mistakes which reflect badly on their organizations and the search processes. In the abstract, it is reasonable to assume that committees will act ethically. However, mistakes happen often enough in searches to warrant preventive measures. The most common problem areas are breaches of confidentiality and inappropriate interview or reference questions, topics discussed further in later chapters.

The chapter on "Organizing an Effective Search Committee" offers suggestions for how the committee can make the values an active part of their process. Values statements reaffirm what an organization stands for, which is helpful for the internal community and an important statement to those who are learning about the organization through the search process.

Vision and the search

Establishing a clear vision is the foundation for developing clear criteria for selecting the next executive director. Clear criteria provide a basis for carefully evaluating candidates and reduce the danger of emphasizing personality over experience and demonstrated success.

When a board develops a clear vision, its dialogues with candidates will be more focused. A very important conversation is to learn whether candidates can share the organization's vision rather than wanting to create a new one or bring one with them. When an executive director has a private vision which is not in sync with the organization, the results are often disastrous and the new leader is usually gone within six months.

The board's role in shaping the vision is described in Chapter Two. The search plan would engage the community in the visioning process to build a shared vision for the organization. Including the constituents has other additional benefits:

- energizing the organization,
- focusing people on creating a better future, and
- providing direction for the search.

When a successful search begins with "visioning," it will more likely conclude with the appointment of the right leader to take the organization to the next level. This is a time to develop dreams which are realistic but also strategic and forward-looking. Exciting goals will attract talented, energetic candidates who want to lead the organization in those efforts. The opposite approach, an invitation to maintain the status quo, will attract candidates who may not be as interested or able to lead in accomplishing major new

When a successful search begins with "visioning," it will more likely conclude with the appointment of the right leader to take the organization to the next level.

goals. Chapter Eleven, "Developing the Profile," elaborates on this theme.

Communication and community

The important message is that there is a plan, everyone will be included and the process has begun.

Making the announcement of the executive director's departure and describing the search plan is the beginning of the public phase which brings the community into the process. Initially, the board can communicate a plan which can be as simple as announcing the chair of the search committee and its membership or the chair and the categories of the members who will serve. Working out the details of the individual members can come later. Also, mentioning that the process will be inclusive, that people will have an opportunity to provide input, will be welcome information even before the dates for those meetings are set. The important message is that there is a plan, everyone will be included and the process has begun.

To the extent possible, this first communication about the search can be a model for sharing information, minimizing anxiety and instilling confidence in the process. An important element is to assure people that this transition is part of the organization's development and can be an opportunity for new growth.

It is always better to proactively state the news, or facts, rather than let rumors and anxiety shape the message.

When there is a reluctance to acknowledge that the head of the organization is leaving, this naturally leads to delays in making the announcement. Having a plan and moving forward as soon as possible is important because it will lessen the time without leadership, or the time without a leader who is fully focused on the organization. If there is a delay in making the announcement and the news leaks out, people's imaginations only heighten the anxiety which occurs during times of change. It is always better to proactively state the news, or facts, rather than let rumors and anxiety shape the message.

Sample search timeline

Figure A (*This is for purposes of illustration, not an absolute.*)

Month 1	Month 2	Month 3	Month 4	Month 5	Month 6
Board preparation and planning	Ads, announcements, networking	Networking continues	Search committee interviews	Finalists' visits	Transition team's work begins
Search committee forms Meet with constituents Develop profile/criteria	Respond to applications	Committee develops questions and prepares to review applications	Comprehensive reference interviews begin	Board decision	New executive director begins meetings before start date
Develop outreach plan		Phone interviews and preliminary references	Recommendations to the board	Transition team meets	

The time frame and preparation for it

The natural course of a thorough search will take four to six months, so it is best to prepare, let people know as soon as possible and begin. That may seem like a surprisingly long time, but it is realistic given the extent of the work to be accomplished. As the chart illustrates, there are many parts of the process and the start of some phases is dependent on the completion of others. The time period covers the board's initial preparations through the identification of candidates, interviews, references, the decision, contract, starting date and the next transition.

Assuming the process will take a minimum of four months, a board has to assess its leadership needs. In some fields, there is a natural rhythm to the year, which includes hiring decisions and contract renewal. Knowing hiring patterns and the length of time an average search takes will help a board assess options for leadership if the current executive director is not available.

If the executive director is leaving suddenly, the board has to devise ways for his or her workload to be covered. A deputy or assistant executive director may be available, or senior managers may be able to divide the work temporarily. Appendix B describes circumstances when having an interim director may be advisable and the process for that search and hiring.

Budget matters

Advertising, long-distance telephone calls, copying and postage are costs each search committee will have. Advertising can be the major expense. There are some unavoidable costs and others which are discretionary, dependent on the resources available. If an organization wants to recruit nationally, it would normally be expected to pay the travel expenses of candidates interviewed initially, and later, the travel expenses of finalists and spouses or partners when they return to meet with the community. If resources are an issue, the search might be limited to candidates in the area. Generally, the organizations pay moving costs for an executive director and his or her family; this could be a predetermined, reasonable amount. Additional costs may be background checks, described in detail in Chapter Nineteen, and consulting advice, should the board seek it, which is discussed in Appendix C.

The search budget would also include expenses for the transition period when the new executive director is in the process of joining the organization. Some of these costs are for trips which the new leader will take for important organizational events and for family trips to find housing, perhaps look at schools for children or employment for a spouse or partner. In addition, the board will have events to introduce the new leader to the immediate community and perhaps to community leaders in the area. Further information can be found in Chapter Twenty One, "The Transition."

Food is an important ingredient in searches. Committees meet a lot. Depending on the budget, food can range from beverages and cookies to brown bag lunches, pot lucks, sandwiches from a local shop or catered meals. When finalists visit (see Chapter Eighteen), there will be additional meetings and food requirements.

The board can determine a budget based on an overview of likely expenses and the organization's resources. This will provide guidance for search committee decisions about expenditures.

Another financial decision is to set a salary range for the next executive director. A range rather than a set amount provides flexibility because candidates may differ widely in years of experience and current salaries. Associations often have data on the compensation of executive directors which can be a resource for the board in setting a salary range. Another resource is the Web site, www.guidestar.com, which provides information about the salaries of executive directors of nonprofit organizations. The Foundation Center's Web site, www.fdncenter.org, has a 990 finder, another resource for understanding comparable salaries. Most relevant are organizations of a similar size and purpose as well as organizations in the same geographic area.

Lengthy notice and retirements

When the head of an organizations retires, a board often has ample notice. When this is the case, the organization should try to avoid selecting a replacement so long in advance that the current leader becomes a "lame duck". On the other hand, there is a distinct advantage to conducting and completing the search before other organizations do, particularly if there is a distinct season of hiring or a lot of competition. The task is to find the right balance.

While moving ahead to give the search process the time it needs, the board should give due deference to the outgoing director. That person may be strong enough not to be viewed as a lame duck initially, but that situation may change as the search process reaches its conclusion. When the search process is nearly concluded and the next executive director is named, the outgoing person often feels neglected because attention is focused on the future and past contributions have a tendency to fade. Sensitivity is required so that both the retiring person and the organization have their needs met.

How planning eases anxiety

Planning, by its nature, requires identifying the important issues and questions. In my experience, boards and search committees are usually nervous at first because they feel the weight of responsibility and face so many unknowns. As they begin to understand the process and take an active role in shaping it they see that they have a real and positive role, which reduces their anxiety enormously.

Planning, by its nature, requires identifying the important issues and questions.

This feeling of being able to understand and influence the process opens the way for other benefits. In the most effective searches, people continue to learn and gain appreciation for the viewpoints of others; using this collective wisdom helps to strengthen each decision. As the search process unfolds, search committees and boards begin to have greater confidence that they are doing justice to their important responsibilities. They know that they are making thoughtful and informed decisions at each step of the process. By the time the search committees prepare their recommendations to the boards, they feel confident that they have made the right choices.

Good planning sets the stage for successful outcomes. The next step is selecting the search committee.

Selecting a Search Committee

This chapter describes the board's role in selecting a search committee and the responsibility and authority of the committee.

Introduction

Selecting the leader of a nonprofit organization is one of the board's most important duties. Therefore, the board wants to assure that there is an excellent search committee to assist it in this critical work.

The committee will have responsibility for creating the description of the organization, its goals and the criteria for the next executive director. It will be gathering community input and communicating regularly with the community. Its work includes advertising and recruiting, evaluating applications and interviewing the most qualified candidates. All of this culminates in the search committee's recommendations of finalists to the board.

A board may want to participate in the selection of committee members, or simply discuss the categories of people who will serve. If the board gives the entire responsibility for picking individuals to the chair, good communication about the goals of the search process and its importance to the community will inform the decisions about committee members.

There was a time when search committees consisted only of board members, and non-board members formed one or more subcommittees or advisory committees. More recently, organizations have learned that a good search is a learning opportunity, greatly enriched by thoughtful and varied perspectives provided by broad representation on the search committee. Advisory committees, described in greater detail at the end of this chapter, were no longer necessary.

Representative search committees work well for organizations that are naturally inclusive and comfortable with the idea, as well as for those who initially doubt this model. Inclusive committees mirror the cultures of most small nonprofits, and those that use them expect them to work well. In my

> Selecting the leader of a nonprofit organization is one of the board's most important duties.

experience, inclusive committees work well even when there are tensions. For example, in organizations where groups were at odds and not communicating, having all constituents represented on the search committees and focused on their common task fostered dialogues which resulted in greater understanding among the different groups.

Selecting the chair of the search committee

The leadership of the search committee is a critical decision for the success of the process and the outcome. It is also an early decision and therefore represents a visible example of how the process will work. When the chair is a respected member of the community, this signals that the community can expect a process which it can trust and respect. Chairs can come from the board, from the staff or active volunteers.

The ideal chair should balance good process and good progress and be adept at moving meetings along respectfully, so that people feel heard.

Much depends on the abilities of the chair as he or she leads the community through this important process. The ideal chair should balance good process and good progress and be adept at moving meetings along respectfully, so that people feel heard. He or she may have to make difficult decisions to maintain the integrity of the search process. This requires the strength to make tough choices and the ability to communicate why the decisions were reached and how they benefit the organization and the search process. In addition, the chair is a model for all the positive attributes of other members of the committee; those attributes are described below. The time element is more demanding for the chair because of the need to oversee coordination and communication.

After the board has selected a chair it would explain its work so far and how that affects the search (if that person is not a board member). Because the board has spent time defining the values which support the search process it should share them with the chair and later with the search committee. The board has also thought about its vision and goals, and this initial meeting may be a good opportunity to share them. Alternatively, the board may want to wait to describe its vision and goals until the search committee begins asking those questions of constituent groups. See Chapter Eleven, "Developing the Profile."

Attributes of search committee members and their responsibilities

Ideal members of the search committee are thoughtful, impartial, committed to the process and respected in the community. They are team players with good judgment. Because the search process is a learning experience in many ways, openness to learning throughout the search will help assure a successful conclusion. And, since the committee may be a candidate's first impression of the organization, each person will also be an ambassador for the organization.

Much that happens within the search committee is confidential, which requires a commitment to confidentiality, particularly in the early stages of the search when the names of candidates are not public. Candidates may withdraw from a search that is not respectful of their need for confidentiality in the initial stages. Their jobs are at stake. Later in the search, confidentiality is critical also. References, search committee discussions and decision-making — all have to remain within the committee.

Because a search takes time, most likely four to six months, committee members have to commit to attending all meetings unless an emergency arises. The committee needs the continuity of the same people present for all discussions. When people miss meetings, perspectives are missing and the dialogues are not the same as they would be with shared experience, analysis and learning. The next chapter, "Organizing an Effective Search Committee," will help in setting up a process which uses the committee's time effectively so people will want to attend all the meetings.

Composition of the committee

At this point, the board has completed its thoughtful planning, which will serve as a model for the search committee chair to be as thorough in thinking about and selecting members of the committee. This means thinking carefully about representation before assembling the committee so the process gets off to a good start. If a committee starts to grow beyond its stated size and composition, there is often a clamor by other individuals and groups for a place at the table. Adding a person later implies that the original committee was somehow deficient, the product of a poorly planned decision. And, if the committee begins growing, the impression is that insistent voices can prevail. The goal is to plan carefully and to establish trust in the

Much that happens within the search committee is confidential, which requires a commitment to confidentiality, particularly in the early stages of the search when the names of candidates are not public.

If a committee starts to grow beyond its stated size and composition, there is often a clamor by other individuals and groups for a place at the table.

integrity of the committee, without everyone feeling that he or she must be present.

The ideal committee has multiple perspectives which encourage better dialogues and continuous learning so that members of the committee get to know and understand the viewpoints of others. Staff gain a better understanding of who the board members are and what concerns them. The board members will have a much better understanding of the staff and program needs. A thoughtful search process provides what is too often a rare opportunity to have these dialogues.

Board members are part of the search committee to provide their perspective, and ultimately it is the board's responsibility to hire the executive director. The board may consult with the chair in asking certain trustees to serve. Ideally, the selection of trustees will represent the broadest thinking about who can contribute to the process. A committee which includes both new and experienced board members can assure a smooth transition to a new leader by combining trustees with a long history with the organization along with newer members who will be the future leadership. A new trustee can intensify his or her involvement and learning through the search process. A long-serving board member, who understands the organization's history and how it developed, represents another valuable perspective.

At times, a board chair is a member of the committee but many feel they cannot make the time commitment. Usually the board's vice-president or president-elect is on the committee to provide continuity because that person will be working closely with the new executive director. If an organization has not determined who will be the next chair of the board, this is the time to make that decision. Serious candidates will want to know.

Typically, a search committee will have representatives from the board, the administration, staff, constituents and perhaps a representative from the community. Each organization should think about representation and desired attributes of committee members based on what best suits the organization's needs.

The size of the committee

There are several reasons why the size of the committee is important. One is the time required for the whole process and the desire to move along at a reasonable pace. A nonprofit organization rightfully wants to be inclusive, and that is possible with a search committee of eight to twelve people. A larger committee, and the difficulty of scheduling any group, tends to prolong the process. Ideally, every person on the committee will attend all interviews. Finding those dates and coordinating them with the candidates' schedules is more difficult than it may appear in the planning phase. Another factor is that near the end of the search, candidates may have competing deadlines because they need to sign a contract with their current employers or are being courted by another organization. A candidate may accept another offer while the search committee is trying to find a date when everyone can meet. This may be hard to imagine at the start of a search, but it could be extremely disappointing if it occurs at the end of the search process.

Another reason why a committee of eight to twelve people is a good size is the informality it can offer. This is the first group a candidate meets, and it may provide his or her first impression of the organization. Developing a rapport with the search committee can be a major factor in retaining a candidate's interest; interviews can appear impersonal if a committee is too large.

Responsibility and authority

Clearly articulated responsibilities ensure a smooth process. Key responsibilities which search committee members assume are: commitment to the values of the organization and those which will guide the search process, attendance and participation at all meetings, and confidentiality during the search as well as after it concludes.

In nonprofits, good practice is to engage whole boards in discussions and decisions based on research and facts prepared by the appropriate committees. Similarly, the search committees can do careful, thoughtful work to recommend options or choices to the boards. The boards use the information provided by the committees as they reach decisions. They will also be meeting the finalists and discussing and analyzing the references before making a selection. Because the boards and their executive directors work so closely together, it is important for the boards to explore the choices thoughtfully and "own" their decisions. Chapter Four discusses this point in more detail.

A nonprofit organization rightfully wants to be inclusive, and that is possible with a search committee of eight to twelve people.

Key responsibilities which search committee members assume are: commitment to the values of the organization and those which will guide the search process, attendance and participation at all meetings, and confidentiality during the search as well as after it concludes.

Advisory committees

While there are trustees on a search committee, the representatives of other constituencies are full participants in the dialogues and decision-making so most nonprofits no longer see a need for advisory committees. Having advisory committees presented several problems. During much of the search process, the identities of candidates are confidential and cannot be shared with other committees. Confidentiality requires that only the search committees interview the candidates initially. This meant that advisory committees had no satisfying role during the confidential phase when the search committees had the primary responsibility and authority. Naturally, people were frustrated and felt they were not on the "real" committees. One advisory committee misunderstood who was actually selecting the next executive director; they thought they were and were angry when they learned that was not the case. Organizations found that rather than isolating secondary committees, a better alternative was to have search committees which included all constituencies.

When there is clarity, good communication and a well-rounded search committee, people will understand and support the concept of one committee. An early announcement can explain how all constituencies will be part of the search committee. This can even precede the naming of individual search committee members, as long as the message is clear that all constituencies will be included.

This chapter has discussed how to think about all the dimensions of creating a search committee. The following chapter is devoted to the smooth functioning of that committee.

Organizing Effective Search Committees

This chapter discusses organization, tasks and the effective use of time.

Introduction

The search committee is ready to begin the work which will be critical to the future of the organization. The committee is probably excited, anxious and somewhat uncertain. The information in this chapter will help the committee better understand its tasks and responsibilities.

Searches require a significant time commitment, in spurts, and require a commitment to be available as needed. The obligation of the chair is to use time wisely and to model that for the committee members. Respecting people's time is important to the process, so that committee members remain committed to attending every meeting. Developing a schedule early, as one of the first steps, helps people plan accordingly. Meeting for a specific purpose (see examples below) uses the committee's time effectively and efficiently. The danger in meeting for the sake of meeting is that it will lessen people's interest in attending regularly.

Search committee members often groan when they first look at the number of meetings. The good news is that people discover that these are important and interesting sessions and that they often get more interesting as the process unfolds. The following sections illustrate the tasks and offer an overview of task-oriented meetings.

The tasks

The search committee has multiple and varied tasks ahead of it. Developing a plan for setting up community meetings, communicating frequently and well, and managing the candidate process are some of the tasks which will help the committee set up its meetings and calendar.

Here is an overview of the search committee's responsibilities/tasks:

- gathering community input, holding meetings so that board, administrators, staff and other constituencies can participate (Chapter Eleven),

- developing the job description, ads and announcements (Chapter Eleven),

- preparing an outreach plan, including networking (Chapter Twelve),

- responding to applications,

- using the criteria to review applications and to select people to interview (Chapter Fourteen),

- planning and carrying out interviews with the most qualified candidates (Chapter Fifteen),

- maintaining confidentiality, discussed in the last portion of this chapter,

- communicating consistently with the community about progress (Chapter Eight),

- conducting references and possibly sharing this work with the board (Chapter Seventeen),

- planning the finalists' visits to the organization (Chapter Eighteen), and

- preparing its report to the board (Chapter Seventeen).

Meetings

When the chair sends out the agenda, well before each meeting, he or she would specify which chapters of the book will provide background for the next discussion.

When the chair sends out the agenda, well before each meeting, he or she would specify which chapters of the book will provide background for the next discussion. Here is an outline explaining how the tasks, outlined above, become the meetings the search committee will need:

- At least one organizational meeting to hear from the board on the committee's charge or responsibility and to hear the board or the board's leadership describe the values which will guide the search; to plan how to gather community input; establish an approximate timeline, begin mapping out a schedule of meetings and have a dialogue about the committee's own views on the organization's strengths and challenges,

- a meeting following the community dialogues to synthesize the input and begin creating the organizational/job description,

- a meeting to review the drafts of the job description, the ad and the announcement, produce final documents and then determine where ads and announcements are placed; strategize networking and make initial assignments,

- a meeting to assess the results of the outreach and strategize next steps and a review of the criteria in preparation for the reading of applications by individual committee members,

- a meeting to review applications,

- probably another meeting to continue reviewing applications and to formulate the interview questions,

- several meetings to interview candidates and a summary meeting to select finalists,

- a meeting to begin preparing the report on finalists for the board,

- a meeting to create a plan for conducting comprehensive references (coordinating this with the board) and the visits of finalists, and

- the final meeting to approve the report to the board.

In addition to these meetings of the full search committee, individual members of the committee will meet with constituent groups at the beginning of the search and attend constituent meetings again when the finalists visit. The full committee could attend these additional meetings but most likely not everyone will be available.

This description of the tasks and how they relate to the meetings will help the committee plan and use its time effectively. Given the amount of work, there are good reasons to have thoughtful dialogues which keep to the agenda in order to accomplish what is needed and to have meetings only when they have a purpose. Setting up a weekly meeting without a specific agenda can dampen enthusiasm. People should come away from a committee meeting feeling it was worth their time because important work was accomplished.

People should come away from a committee meeting feeling it was worth their time because important work was accomplished.

The meetings, described above, are an overview, based on experience, but not an absolute. It may be that some meetings can combine several tasks or that some tasks require additional meetings. It could be that more meetings are necessary for reasons which cannot be predicted at the start of the process. The number of meetings which are necessary will become clearer as the committee begins its work.

Search committee planning and logistics

Once the chair and committee are in place, they can develop an overall timeline which should provide flexibility for the unseen but give a general overview of the process and a target conclusion date. Communicating this to the community, along with the introduction of the search committee, is another means of reducing the mystery and anxiety.

Some things make a search process take longer. In particular, trying to schedule around winter holidays or the summer vacation season is very difficult. Having a very large search committee, more than ten or twelve people, will complicate the scheduling of meetings further.

Setting up a full schedule as early as possible maximizes the attendance of search committee members so that everyone on the committee is present to participate in discussions and decisions. The chair should convey the time requirements and the importance of attendance before committee members accept. If, at the beginning of the process, some people realize they cannot make the time commitment, there is still time to select others to assure continuity on the committee.

Some of the ways to have effective, efficient and well-attended meetings are:

- provide a clear agenda which people receive in advance of the meeting,
- begin and end meetings on time,
- encourage healthy dialogues but keep focused on goals and tasks,
- meet only when there is something substantial to discuss,
- summarize at the end of each meeting, so people understand the next steps, and
- send out a written reminder including who will do what by when.

Confidentiality

This is a topic which always needs discussion because committee members are usually uncomfortable and unsure about how to handle questions from people outside the committee. Naturally, members of the community are curious and will ask search committee members for information. This curiosity can be satisfied, in part, by frequent communication about the progress of the search process. See Chapter Eight. Committee members can restate what has been communicated but cannot divulge confidential information such as the names of candidates, the results of references or how decisions occurred.

It can be helpful for committee members and the community to be reminded that the entire community will have an opportunity to meet the finalists later in the process. Another important reminder is that only the identities of finalists are made public. The names of all other candidates are never shared because it may cause them embarrassment or jeopardize their current employment.

The following guidelines may help committee members respond comfortably. Beyond public information, a committee member can say "Much of the work of the committee is confidential at this point" or "I am not at liberty to discuss that." These statements are consistent with the message to the community at the start of the search and in follow-up communications. When in doubt, a search committee member can refer questions to the chair, which assures consistency and is particularly important in delicate or difficult situations.

Confidentiality also requires some logistical decisions. Applications sent to the chair, rather than to the organization, assure confidentiality initially. Because correspondence with candidates has to be confidential, as well, that also becomes the task of the chair or someone he or she appoints.

This chapter explained the tasks and the purposes of meetings so that a committee can anticipate its responsibilities and the time commitment. The following chapter on ethical and legal obligations supports the committee's commitment to the organization's values.

Legal and Ethical Obligations

This chapter describes the ethical values and legal obligations which ensure the integrity of the search process.

Introduction

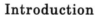

"Why devote a whole chapter to the subject?" is a question a board may ask.

"Why devote a whole chapter to the subject?" is a question a board may ask. The purpose of a separate chapter is to emphasize the importance of the issues and also to provide a thorough resource where people can easily find answers. While the topics covered here are mentioned in other parts of the book, this chapter provides a complete discussion, in one place, of the important legal and ethical topics which arise in a search.

The foundation is the mission statement and values which guide each non-profit; the search process itself should reflect those same values. This is the opportunity to highlight the organization's values for everyone who hears about the search. A well-planned process will involve people at all levels within the organization and a great number of people externally.

While the internal community has opportunities to know the values, seeing their application in a search process illustrates those commitments again. People outside the organization may understand the values well, somewhat, or not at all. Chapters Two and Seven have suggestions for developing values statements for the search. While this chapter is concerned with ethical and legal obligations, doing the right thing also means that people — both those in the community and those who learn about the organization during the search process — will feel good about the process.

In addition to ethical considerations, there are legal guidelines. The Federal Equal Employment Opportunity laws can be found at http://www.eeoc.gov. This site also has information about questions which are not acceptable in interviews. Using these guidelines the search committee can develop acceptable questions based on the organization's goals and criteria and make a commitment to asking each candidate the same set of questions. Developing questions is discussed at greater length in Chapter Sixteen, "Interviews."

The Web sites for individual states are another resource for legal guidance which will have specific information about the state's anti-discrimination laws. Some state laws are broader than federal laws, for example, prohibiting discrimination based on sexual preference. State regulations may also apply to organizations with fewer numbers of employees than federal laws do.

An overview of issues which affect the integrity of the process

The integrity of the process is critical to a successful search and transition. When people view the process as fair, they will respect the board's decision and unite behind it. To assure the integrity of the process, several issues need to be discussed, resolved and clearly communicated. Once there are public announcements the board and the search committee should feel bound by them, which means, of course, that they should be very thoughtful and careful before making public announcements.

The integrity of the process is critical to a successful search and transition.

At least four issues can cause people to question the integrity of the process:

- Changing the job requirements. Later in this chapter, is a section which can serve as a guide to search committees as they develop the written job description, which includes both minimum requirements and preferred qualifications.

- Adding people to the search committee after it is constituted and announced publicly. For that reason, Chapter Five, "Selecting the Search Committee," provides guidance and encourages thoughtfulness before any announcement is made.

- Having search committee members who begin participating in committee work and then decide they want to become candidates. That can be avoided by an early, public announcement that serving on the search committee is a statement that the person is not a candidate. The chair can make that clear to each prospective search committee member before he or she accepts the invitation to serve. While there may well be people in the organization interested in becoming candidates, he or she should not serve on the committee and should apply at the appropriate time before the stated deadline.

- Having a trustee or staff member announce his or her candidacy after the selection and announcement of finalists. All internal candidates are welcome to apply according to the public deadline. After the announced deadline new candidates can only enter the process if the search is publicly reopened to all, which means re-advertising as well.

The process itself should be clearly communicated at the beginning with updates in the course of the search. When a search committee adopts its timeline, that information should be public. To provide flexibility, the committee may want to state that its goal is to complete the process by a certain date but that the search will continue until the board has strong choices. It is possible that unforeseen events will delay the process. In that case, the committee would communicate the amended timeline. When the search committee is certain of the closing date for applications, that date is communicated publicly.

The search committee

The formation of the search committee will be an early indication of the values which will govern the process.

The formation of the search committee will be an early indication of the values which will govern the process. Respect for the search committee translates into confidence that this will be a fair process. Having a balance of roles — board, staff, and constituents — will assure that all perspectives are heard and will convey the commitment to inclusion. Gender balance, diversity and age balance (including number of years with the organization) will provide additional viewpoints and a more balanced perspective on the whole organization.

At the beginning of the search committee's work, the committee chair or the board chair can present the committee with the board's statement on values for the search process. If there is a member of the committee, or the board, who is a human resources professional, he or she can add perspective by describing the practicalities of values, ethics and legalities and how they apply to the process. The Web site, www.eeoc.gov, or a specific state's Web site, are helpful places to seek additional information or might substitute if a human resources professional is not available. As the committee discusses the board's values and its role in the search, the ethical and legal issues become more real. Throughout the process, the chair and the search committee can develop the habit of examining and discussing proposed questions and actions to assure that they are fair. The results or decisions concerning values, ethics or legalities can be documented to provide a valuable resource as the search continues and can be included in communications about the search process.

Defining the criteria for an executive director

Introduction

Careful thought is required in developing the document which describes the organization, its goals and the criteria for the next executive director to assure that it represents the values the organization embraces. When the mission and values of the organization are clear, prospective candidates can assess the "fit" with their own values.

Developing the statement of qualifications is more difficult than it might appear because, at the beginning of the search process, the committee will have high hopes of finding the ideal candidates who possess every imaginable attribute and extraordinary experience. In reality, the candidates will most likely be variations of the "ideal," not an exact match. At the end of the search people will logically compare the stated qualifications and the experience of the finalists. Clarity is important.

The required qualifications should be clear, based on the organization's mission and goals, and not subject to change. Once the qualifications are put in writing they are the basis for evaluating candidates, so great care is important in developing and stating those criteria. The following examples explain how to think about the necessary qualifications.

Once the qualifications are put in writing they are the basis for evaluating candidates, so great care is important in developing and stating those criteria.

Requirements and preferences

The goal is to be very clear about the minimum requirements and retain flexibility about "preferred" qualifications. In describing desired experience, it is important to separate requirements from preferences. Clear statements about education or credentialing requirements will help potential candidates as well as the committee itself when it begins to evaluate applications. An example is: "A master's degree is required and a doctorate is preferred."

Minimum years of experience required in the field or as an administrator can be a baseline criteria. This might appear as "At least five years of leadership experience in a human services organization is required." If the organization is open to considering candidates from fields other than the obvious one, it should state that. An example might be: "We will consider candidates with degrees and administrative experience in social work, but we are also open to candidates from allied fields."

An area that often causes problems is fund-raising. Most nonprofits expect an executive director to assist the board in fund-raising. Many candidates ready for their first leadership role may not have actual experience in fund-raising but usually have some exposure to it and a willingness to do it. Someone who is already an executive director most likely will have the experience, but not every organization is large enough to have current executive directors as candidates.

Wording the job description carefully is important because if the requirements are narrowly defined, it may be more limiting later than the committee anticipates at the formulating and writing stage.

Many search committees start with the notion that fund-raising experience is crucial but then are attracted to candidates who have everything but that experience. Depending on the absolute needs and the size of the organization (which may influence the requirements for candidates' experience), the job description could state: "Fund-raising experience is preferred" or "Fund-raising experience is required." The committee should be certain about this before committing to it in the final document. Wording the job description carefully is important because if the requirements are narrowly defined, it may be more limiting later than the committee anticipates at the formulating and writing stage.

In writing the description, it is best for the committee to try to avoid unnecessary limitations. It is very possible that the search committee will find terrific candidates who would be ready to move into an executive director's job for the first time but who lack experience in some areas that an experienced executive director would have. The right mix of requirements and flexibility in the job description will permit a committee to have discretion later. While the need for flexibility may be difficult to envision at the start of the process, it can become an issue later when the committee meets actual candidates. An organization begins with a picture of the "ideal" candidates and then finds that the applicants are variations of that "ideal"— so it is best to avoid too many restrictions.

Having a small number of basic requirements and a longer list of preferences is a good balance. When the search committee sets up the minimum criteria those criteria also serve as a basis for evaluating applications. As the committee has this dialogue about minimum requirements, they continually refine their thinking about what the organization absolutely needs and where support mechanisms exist in areas where candidates have a learning curve. The "preferred" categories provide flexibility in evaluating candidates who may bring other assets.

Being certain about the minimum requirements assures that the committee judges applications fairly and consistently. For example, if the public statement is: "The next executive director must have experience in an urban, diverse organization," that becomes one of the minimum requirements. Candidates will understand if the search committee states that they do not meet the minimum criteria. They would not be understanding, and would not have been treated fairly, if the rejection stated or implied that the committee changed its mind about the minimum criteria or if the person hired does not meet those criteria.

A committee should be very certain about how to describe the minimum requirements before the job description is final or becomes public. If there is doubt on a particular topic, having it in the "preferred" category provides flexibility. This permits a committee to interview or select a candidate whose other qualifications they could not initially foresee. Flexibility is helpful because the search process is a learning experience; the only certainty is that there will be surprises and dilemmas no one can predict ahead of time. Chapter Eleven, "Developing the Written Description," explains how these criteria are included in the written piece which the search committee creates.

Advertising

Since the basis of the ad will be the job description, the suggestions about care in wording are the same. Required and preferred categories make the ad clear, understandable and flexible. Chapter Twelve, "Forms of Outreach," explains how to develop the advertisement.

Confidentiality

It is unethical to make public the names of candidates without their permission. In the initial stages, when both parties are checking the feasibility of the match, candidates may request, and deserve, confidentiality. A breach can jeopardize an individual's job, cause a candidate to withdraw and reflect badly on the process and the organization. Only the search committee ever knows the identities of all candidates. While a candidate may choose to let people beyond the search committee know (this is particularly true of internal candidates), the best response from the search committee is: "We are not at liberty to say who has applied." When candidates are selected as finalists, they must give permission to make their candidacies public. At that

It is unethical to make public the names of candidates without their permission.

time, they will be notifying their employers, meeting constituents and agreeing to have people call their references.

Interviews

In order to be equitable, the search committee develops its questions ahead of time and asks each candidate the same set of questions. Those questions address professional experience, particularly as it relates to the goals of the organization. Most often the questions flow directly from the goals and requirements contained in the written description.

When the search committee chooses candidates for interviews, it has determined that the candidates meet the minimum requirements. Therefore, questions should be appropriately respectful of current and prior experience.

When the search committee chooses candidates for interviews, it has determined that the candidates meet the minimum requirements. Therefore, questions should be appropriately respectful of current and prior experience. As an example, if the ad read "fund-raising experience is preferred," a committee would not tell a candidate that the lack of such experience is a deficit because the decision was made that it was not an absolute requirement. Instead, the committee could inquire about the candidate's knowledge of fund-raising, opening the way to also learn about his or her appetite for it.

Some questions are simply illegal. Examples are: personal questions such as age, marital status, sexual preference, and number of children or plans to have them. When in doubt about the legality of questions, a committee could consult the EEOC Web site, its state's Web site and other human resource or nonprofit sites that address the legal aspects of interviewing and hiring. Or, the committee could consult knowledgeable board members, a lawyer or associations to which the organization belongs.

The search committee's task is to develop questions which are professional and respectful. Before the interviews, the chair of the search committee should deliver a clear message that "trick" questions or impromptu ones are unacceptable. Unplanned questions can be inappropriate, unfriendly, insulting, unethical and illegal. These problematical questions are different than simple follow-up questions to clarify a point or build on it.

Some of these suggestions may seem self-evident, but being clear up-front avoids problems. These issues are being emphasized because mistakes have occurred and ultimately reflected badly on the organizations.

References

Like interview questions, reference inquiries concern professional competence and the ability to successfully fill the job requirements. A set of reference questions, asked about each candidate, will assure equity. A human resources professional or a lawyer could review them to assure that they are appropriate. See Chapter Nineteen on the topic of references for a broader perspective. The content and results of references are always confidential and seen only by the board and in some cases by the search committee.

By the time reference interviews occur, there should be no question that the candidate meets the minimum criteria. Therefore, questions of references should always be respectful of a candidate's experience. Again, this may seem self-evident, but unfortunately some search committee members take on the role of tough investigators and ask inappropriate questions. Perhaps they feel they did not know how to uncover "the truth" in a previous search and carry that concern into this new situation. The result is that references, who feel the questions have been inappropriate or demeaning, will usually tell this to the candidate. Candidates, thus insulted, will usually withdraw from the search, which is a loss for the organization and does not reflect well upon it.

The purpose of the reference calls is to learn more about the challenges the candidates have had, their success in solving them and their leadership style. The questions are designed to obtain more information for the committee and the board, but again they should be respectful and never belittle the candidates' experience. This does not mean that a call to a reference cannot be informative. These calls are meant to enrich the organization's understanding of candidates. The information on references in Chapter Nineteen will explain how to conduct thorough reference interviews in a way which provides the committee and the board with the information they need.

Contracts

Many boards have trustees who are lawyers, or they have legal counsel for the organization who can be a source of contract information and sample contracts. Some associations collect data on contracts which they will share with members. They may also have samples or guidelines. Since the contract represents a major commitment for the organization, a lawyer should review the final document. Many candidates will also have a lawyer review the contract and may suggest areas they want to include.

Basic areas covered in contracts are:

- compensation,
- moving costs (if applicable),
- housing and housing allowances (if applicable),
- terms of employment,
- how extension of the contract will be determined,
- description of duties and goals from the search committee's job description (priorities or goals can be the topic of the first board/executive director workshop or meeting, and new goals can be added each year),
- evaluation process and a schedule for it, and
- termination agreements.

Chapter Twenty has more information on compensation packages and contracts.

Goals and the contract

The search committee gathered input from all constituencies to clearly articulate the next set of goals for the organization. This can be the basis for the first year's annual goals if there are no unforeseen changes by the time the new executive director arrives. Most likely the goals articulated were for a longer term. The board and its new executive director can have a fruitful dialogue about the priorities: what can reasonably be completed in the first year, what will be started, and which items are a lower priority in the first years or depend upon the completion of initial goals. There can be an agreement in the contract to develop concrete goals in a stated time period and to add this material as a supplement.

Putting these agreements about goals and priorities in a document assures their availability in order to check on progress. This document is a useful addition to the contract because it is specific. Vague goals, which could apply to any organization, fail to provide specific and measurable objectives. A statement such as "carries out the duties as directed by the board" does not provide focus or goals and would be difficult to evaluate. Each year an updated list of goals can be added. This concrete goal-setting becomes the basis for monthly conversations about progress and annual, formal evaluations of the executive director and the board.

Chapter Twenty One, on the transition to new leadership, discusses developing a constructive evaluation process for the executive director and for the board.

Reopening a search

In the event that a search fails to produce candidates acceptable to the board or candidates who will accept the job, the organization will need to reopen the search, place new advertisements and make other public announcements.

The suggestions in this book about being sure the finalists are strong and keeping the lines of communication open about other deadlines or competition may avoid a failure. However, searches are complicated and people are complex so the unpredictable can happen.

While this situation is a setback, in the long term hiring the right person remains the most important goal. Anxiety and disappointment may cause people to want a quick solution, which may have some appeal but may also be the wrong long-term solution. Acknowledging the disappointment and then moving beyond it is the right decision and long-term, the organization will benefit by finding a short-term solution and beginning the process again.

To the extent possible the board chair can explain why it is necessary to reopen the search. One reason, which can certainly be public, is that the board's choice accepted another offer. The implication is that the board chose to reopen the search rather than select one of the remaining finalists. If the situation occurred because there were negative results from the final references or a disappointing visit to a finalist's organization, the board chair can simply say that there were issues which stood in the way of concluding the search. It is difficult to have to make this announcement, but it is preferable to a bad decision which everyone will regret later.

A quick solution such as hiring a candidate who does not meet the criteria would undermine the integrity of the search process; the same is true of hiring someone who was not part of the original search. While having to reopen the search is a disappointment, the decision is too important to settle for less than the ideal. That message is the one constituents need   to hear.

This chapter has presented information on legal and ethical obligations. The next chapter discusses the importance of communication throughout the process.

Communication

This chapter emphasizes how thoughtful communication can support the organization through the leadership transition.

A reminder of why it is important

Most people find change anxiety-provoking. A change in the leadership of an organization will make every constituent group uneasy. The board worries that the organization will lose ground. It worries about the responsibility of hiring really well. The board worries that funders and clients will be uncomfortable during the transition. Staff will wonder how well they will like the new executive director and how much the organization will change. Because the head of the organization shapes the work and the climate, staff will worry about both and about the security of their jobs.

Chapter Four describes why communication by the board is important in the early stages of the search, both to acknowledge the anxiety and to explain the plan. Because the search will continue over a number of months, regular updates help community members understand the work that is being done by the search committee, especially during the confidential phase of the search when constituents will feel disconnected. The goal is to have consistent communication throughout the search, sharing appropriate information about the progress and the process. The communication chart, at the end of the chapter, is a way to assure that everyone is hearing about the search process at least once a month.

Responsibility for communicating

The board begins the communication cycle at the start of the search and ends it with the announcement of the next executive director. Chapter Two has a discussion of positive messages the board can relay to constituents at the beginning of the search, including the themes of continuity and opportunity. When the board has selected a search committee chair, that person assumes responsibility for communicating about the search process.

While the search committee is actively engaged in their work, other people are wondering what is happening. The communication chart illustrates one way to assure that information, written or oral, is getting to all constituencies at every phase of the search. Written information can be included in a regularly scheduled newsletter or other mailing. More and more, Web sites keep constituents informed about the progress of a search. Staff meetings or board meetings are a natural time for an update by the chair of the search committee. While it may seem sufficient to have a staff or faculty member report at their meetings, the presence of the chair is an added tension-reducing message and conveys the search committee's desire to keep the community informed.

The content of the information

The information reflects the course of the search. Initially, there will be an announcement that the head or executive director is leaving. When the board conveys that this transition is another step in the development of the organization, the loss of the leader is not as jarring. The best scenario is if the board is ready to talk about the next steps. People will be less anxious when they hear concrete plans. The announcement can be as simple as saying that the board is selecting a search committee which will represent all the constituencies of the organization and that there will be forums where everyone will have the opportunity to share their thoughts and concerns.

The next announcement can simply be introducing the members of the search committee. Periodically, there can be information on the progress of various aspects of the search, such as the advertising, timeline, a sense of the number of applicants, where they are from (geographically) and their current roles (but not their names). For communication planning, the phases of the search dictate the extent of information about candidates. The identity of candidates is not public until the finalist phase and constituents need to be reminded of that, but constituents also deserve frequent updates on progress.

Confidentiality

Because confidentiality is so important, it is helpful to have frequent reminders as well as explanations about why this is important. The primary reason is that releasing a candidate's name before that person gives permission can harm his or her career.

It is understandable that when a candidate is initially investigating whether or not there is a good fit with the organization, he or she may not want to make their interest public. Early in the search, frequent updates to constituents will have to substitute for specifics of candidate identity. Having a sense of how the process is progressing makes it easier for constituents to forego knowing the names of applicants. That situation changes when the candidates and the organization are more serious and finalists are announced.

Until the search committee has narrowed the candidates down to a small number of finalists, the names of all candidates should remain confidential. The names of candidates who do not become finalists are never revealed because this might jeopardize their current employment. Finalists, on the other hand, have made the decision to make their candidacy public and have given permission for the search committee to call references. Chapter Eighteen explains further how confidentiality is different when candidates accept the invitation to be finalists.

The names of candidates who do not become finalists are never revealed because this might jeopardize their current employment.

The confidentiality issue is important enough to repeat here and in an organization's communication updates. Only the names of the finalists are made public. The identities of all other candidates are known only to the search committee and those names are never shared. For this reason, applications are sent to the search committee chair and acknowledged through the committee, not the organization. That simple procedure also signals to candidates that the committee understands the need for confidentiality.

Communicating with candidates

Throughout the search process, communication with candidates is important as a courtesy to applicants; it also reflects positively on the organization. A simple acknowledgment of an application along with a sense of the timeline is the first step. To maintain confidentiality, correspondence always goes to a candidate's home address. If there are delays or changes, the candidates should know. After the search committee has reviewed applications and knows that some people do not meet the basic criteria, a letter can be sent thanking them for their interest but explaining that they will not be interviewed. This practice is more considerate than waiting months, until the search is completed, to let applicants know. After reviewing applications, the nonprofit would send qualified candidates a completed description of the organization, its goals and the role of the next executive director, if they have not already done that.

When the search committee selects finalists, this is the time to thank and notify other candidates, those interviewed and those who may be in a "hold" group. If there is an internal candidate who will not become a finalist, the search committee chair can notify him or her personally. For candidates interviewed, and finalists not selected, a personal call is always preferable — in addition to a letter of appreciation.

Communicating in the finalist phase

The search committee chair is most likely the person who will describe the finalists to different groups within the community. A useful part of the discussion is to share how the search committee believes that each finalist's qualifications, skills, experience and other qualities will enable him or her to lead the organization in accomplishing the stated goals. The chair will also explain the purpose of these visits.

The finalists' visits have multiple purposes, and it is important to be aware of this and to handle everyone's needs thoughtfully. Good communication, at this point, acknowledges that the nonprofit's constituency wants to learn more about the finalists and simultaneously that candidates are seeking more information. Chapter Eighteen has more on the dual purposes of the visit.

When finalists meet the community, a short biography is a useful introduction. A search committee member can develop two paragraphs for each person, covering work experience and education. The board will usually want to see more extensive information: the résumé, cover letter and supporting documents. If staff would like to see the full résumé, particularly if that has been the norm in other searches, the search committee would ask the candidates' permission first. If they agree, it can be available in a central location.

Finalists want more information about the organization, both from written materials and from the people who make up the organization. Candidates seriously contemplating a new leadership role will ask to see reports such as financial audits, annual reports, board bylaws, feasibility studies and evaluation reports. The search committee can anticipate these requests and prepare the same packages of information for each finalist. This is discussed further in Chapter Eighteen.

Conveying the decision

When the board selects the next leader and that person accepts, the communication enters a new phase. The search committee is the next to hear. Some groups, staff for instance, would be notified soon thereafter, ideally by the board and search committee chairs. All of the constituents who have been receiving search information should be on the announcement list.

Because this is also an opportunity for positive public relations, it is worth strategizing on how to maximize the effect. There might be notices in journals, newspapers, association literature — all opportunities to gain recognition for the organization. Announcements can go to current and former donors, friends of the nonprofit and volunteers. Another group, to notify and thank, are people who were helpful during the search, who shared resources, recommended candidates or provided helpful references.

The selection of a new executive director is a major event; the organization will want to notify everyone who could be interested. Assembling this list is best completed ahead of the search closing so the news is distributed quickly.

Because this is also an opportunity for positive public relations, it is worth strategizing on how to maximize the effect.

Search Communication
Figure B

	Month 1	Month 2	Month 3	Month 4	Month 5	Month 6
Board						
Meeting*						
Written**						
Person***						
Staff						
Meeting						
Written						
Person						
Friends						
Meeting						
Written						
Person						
Funders						
Meeting						
Written						
Person						
Other						
Meeting						
Written						
Person						

* Meeting – A faculty or board meeting, constituents or other group
** Written – Note if it is a newsletter, letter, Web site or other publication.
*** Person – Person responsible for a written update or attending a meeting.

How Leadership Needs Change

This chapter describes how leadership needs change as organizations grow and develop, and the unique challenges posed by the departure of a founder or long-serving leader.

Introduction

In working with many different nonprofits over a period of more than 20 years, I noticed some patterns which seem to be linked to how long the organization had existed. While each organization has its own history, culture and personality, these patterns can be useful as a nonprofit assesses where it is and how it wants to develop further.

These insights about organizations at different stages of development are the result of working with nonprofits whose reasons for leadership searches varied widely. Several startups were hiring their first executive directors. At the other extreme were nonprofits which were replacing influential founders or long-term leaders who seemed inseparable from the organizations. In the mid-range were organizations whose leaders had been there for ten to fifteen years. At the other end of the spectrum were nonprofits which struggled with frequent turnover, something the boards needed to understand before they could successfully change that pattern.

The issues highlighted in this chapter play an important role at the start of the search but can easily be overlooked when there is so much to do. Thinking about how leadership needs change as nonprofits mature and develop can help boards and search committees understand how those changes affect the leadership skills needed at a particular time.

Hiring the first executive director

When a board is looking for its first executive director, the size of the organization and its immediate tasks/goals will naturally influence the experience, qualities and characteristics of the person they are seeking. A successful leader of a young nonprofit is often passionate, energetic and an articulate visionary. These are useful qualities for persuading funders and staff to make

While each organization has its own history, culture and personality, these patterns can be useful as a nonprofit assesses where it is and how it wants to develop further.

The issues highlighted in this chapter play an important role at the start of the search but can easily be overlooked when there is so much to do.

a commitment to a nonprofit with no track record. A new organization is small enough so that a visionary leader can know the details of the operation first-hand without being overly burdened with administrative work. He or she can devote energy to the exciting work of creating this new organization.

Someone who excels in the start-up phase has very special talents. He or she may make the transition to leading a larger organization but may not have the interest in the operational side or the management skills to continue to build an organization as it grows over time. A founding executive director may feel too removed from the programs and too burdened with administration. As a nonprofit grows, he or she can find the role less fulfilling and less suited to their talents.

Transitioning to the second executive director

Initially this transition may be difficult because the long-term leader is reluctant to face a change in his or her role, or because the board and staff cannot imagine the organization without the leadership of that person.

At some point the board, or the founding executive director, recognizes the need to build the organization, to grow its programs and its impact. They also realize that this requires a thoughtful transition plan so that the nonprofit will succeed beyond the founding executive director and the original board. This requires a conscious shift, moving away from personalities towards developing the organization's identity separately from that of the early leadership. It also requires a willingness to believe that others can identify with the mission, protect it and help it grow. For people who have committed their heart and soul to a nonprofit and its mission, this shift will not be easy. Initially this transition may be difficult because the long-term leader is reluctant to face a change in his or her role, or because the board and staff cannot imagine the organization without the leadership of that person.

For the board, this change requires thoughtfulness and sensitivity as it works on the issue of transition, while respecting the dedication of the founder and trying to help that person feel comfortable about changing his or her role. There are several possible options, but no one solution works for every situation.

Someone who has dedicated his or her life to an organization may need a final project to mark the transition. This might be to work on a specific fund-raising effort with long-term supporters. Often nonprofits honor a long-serving leader with a commemorative event. One executive director chose to write a history of the organization after retiring. Another departing leader thoughtfully left two notebooks for the next person. One detailed deadlines and contractual obligations; the other provided a more informal overview of how things worked and the out-going leader's perspective on the next priorities. The board can be most helpful to someone who is leaving by opening the dialogue about ways to ease the transition.

In some organizations, a visionary leader has willingly relinquished operational responsibilities to concentrate on external relations or board or donor development. That is a difficult transition which only a few organizations have managed successfully. In other situations, leaders were comfortable with their decision to retire, believing that the boards would provide continuity and wisely select new leaders to assure that the visions endure.

Continuing an organization's important work is a worthy goal. This transition from a founder or a leader who has served for decades requires great wisdom from the board to figure out what works best for the nonprofit and for its out-going leader. The danger in not resolving this transition or leadership succession is that a valuable organization can fail to outlive its founders, a great loss because the work or the cause often loses its strongest champions.

The danger in not resolving this transition or leadership succession is that a valuable organization can fail to outlive its founders, a great loss because the work or the cause often loses its strongest champions.

At times a leader is simply ready to retire. One co-founder, who had been the co-head of a school for thirty-three years, understood the need for the organization to move forward. He and his co-head announced their retirement to the board several years in advance so that the board would have adequate planning time. After the interview with the person who would become the next head, this co-founder said: "I like him the best because he will take this organization the farthest."

His statement demonstrated that he was ready to see the organization not only continue its work, but grow and develop in new ways. Successful leadership requires selflessness — the desire to see the organization flourish beyond one's own tenure.

Another nonprofit had been very anxious about hiring "an outsider" for the first time after the long tenure of the founders followed by a nineteen year tenure of someone who "grew up" in the organization. The comment of the board chair illustrates the positive aspects of that transition:

> "Our new executive director has convinced people that this is a different but better institution. We are no longer trying to capture the glorious past."

The mission remained the same, but that insight about organizational changes and "a different but better institution" freed people to assess how well the programs were meeting current needs. They were able to evaluate their work in order to continue building "a better institution." Change is inevitable; when the process is thoughtfully managed it can strengthen the organization and its faith in itself.

After a long leadership tenure, a board which has been largely supportive and responsive faces a very different role. This transition to new leadership requires that the board become more proactive in guiding the new leader and the organization. Because this is a major shift in the board's role, it needs to dedicate time to addressing the necessary changes directly and thoughtfully. This work can be accomplished outside of regular board meetings through workshops or retreats where professional development and the board's evolving role are the focus. Board-building after an executive director's long tenure is also discussed in Chapter Three.

Hiring leaders for more mature nonprofits

While the leader of a young nonprofit possesses vision and sufficient management skills for a small organization, in a more mature organization the balance of vision and management may shift. This may mean that the executive director's role is to be a strong spokesperson, to focus on external relations and fundraising and less on operational issues, or programs, at a hands-on level. As the search committee of a mature organization assesses its needs, and the other staff who are available to manage some areas, it can create a job description which specifically fits the current circumstances and the balance of responsibilities.

A more mature organization will have a larger number of staff and most likely more experienced senior staff. Nonetheless, the executive director has to understand the financial, programmatic and operational parts to assure his or her credibility, and the credibility of the entire organization. The executive director of a mature organization usually has different interests and skill sets than the first executive director. He or she has less time to devote to program areas but wants to support the board and the organization in planning the future and assuring that funding is available to achieve the vision. The following chapter on leadership provides insights into the combination of leadership and management skills that an executive director needs.

Organizations which have experienced frequent turnover

Frequent turnover at the executive director's level can have many causes. Not recognizing the significance of organizational change or growth, and failing to adequately prepare for it, can be one reason. Another cause might be a limited outreach which resulted in weak choices. Or, the problem might be faulty references. Other chapters describe how to have an effective outreach and how to conduct thorough references. The emphasis in this discussion is on the organizational reasons for frequent turnover.

One organization had ten leaders in thirteen years. They just kept hiring the same sort of person, with similar experience and leadership capacities, — ten times. The next search began with a series of questions which revealed how completely their client base had changed and how unprepared the board and staff were to deal with this new reality. The board finally understood that they needed an executive director who could help the board and staff develop the skills to serve the new client base. The next executive director succeeded because she was the right person to meet the new challenges.

As a board and a search committee define the needs of its organization, it is critical to look carefully at the realities of the current situation and to anticipate future directions. A search committee would want to separate itself from the needs, or job description, that were used when the prior leader was hired. This is a new occasion and a new opportunity.

The beginning of the search is the right time to take a closer look at the organization, both to take pride in its strengths and accomplishments and to honestly assess what its weaknesses are. Chapter Eleven describes how to look at the organization and its needs so that the search and the hiring are informed by a knowledgeable, and current, assessment. If a nonprofit remains uncertain about why previous directors failed, this is the time to find expert advice through a funder or a technical assistance organization so that the next search is successful.

This chapter introduced the concept of changing leadership needs as an organization grows and develops. The following chapter describes attributes of leadership.

Attributes of Leadership

This chapter provides a summary of leadership concepts so that an organization can assess its needs and the capabilities of candidates.

Introduction

Many experts have devoted books to in-depth discussions of leadership theories. This chapter provides a brief, practical overview designed to prepare a search committee and a board by introducing some dimensions of leadership as background for their work.

The more a search committee understands leadership qualities and the candidates, the more likely their decisions will be solid ones. Each of the following sections identifies key leadership qualities and skills and explains how to use this information to learn more about candidates in interviews and when speaking with references.

The ability to inspire and develop relationships

The ability to inspire and develop strong relationships with each constituent group is an important attribute for an executive director because the work of a nonprofit happens through its board members, administrators, staff and funders. In an interview setting, passion about the meaning of his or her work is the first indicator of a candidate's potential ability to inspire and motivate others.

As a leader communicates what he or she cares about and why the organization's mission matters, this commitment inspires others and also serves to reinforce everyone's focus on the goals. The interviews with the committee are an introduction to this topic, and a search committee will want to learn more about candidates' relationships through reference interviews.

Most leaders also care deeply about their staff. They know people as individuals; know their strengths, where he or she needs to grow and what each cares about. They know intuitively that nonprofit organizations fulfill their promise through people; effective leaders show appreciation for staff contributions. Through their genuine sensitivity to others, leaders build strong relationships with staff, with their board and with external constituencies. Interviews with candidates will begin to illustrate their relationships, and the search committee can use the references to learn more.

Mission mesh

People choose to work in the nonprofit world because they want to make a difference in the lives of others. The long hours required to accomplish goals matter less when there is a genuine match between the person and the mission. These comments from one leader illustrate the point:

> *"I would advise someone that it's a whole life. This job is as much recreation for me as it is a vocation. I don't need to escape. Every once in a while I just need to rest."*

Personal histories reveal what people care about and what their values are. When a search committee provides the opportunity for candidates to tell their stories, the committee will begin to hear how deeply someone cares about the work. A search committee will also want to hear if an individual's values match the mission of the organization. Chapter Fifteen has guidance on open-ended but focused questions to accomplish this.

While this book primarily deals with searches for executive directors, the "mission mesh" is important in other roles as well. One executive director of an environmental organization felt that an interest in the environment was not necessary in hiring a business manager. The person who was hired had no prior work experience, or personal interest, in environmental issues. After a year, the business manager left for a job in workforce development, an area of prior interest. "Mission mesh" does give meaning. When personal interests dovetail with work, people feel more commitment to the organization and greater fulfillment through their work.

Many excellent leaders gain experience as leaders and managers in one field while devoting personal time to a different field. When their non-work interests mesh with an organization's mission the result can be a good fit. The same is true for staff. One executive director was an ardent environmentalist who happened to be a long-tenured head of a nonprofit whose focus was music. Applying to be the executive director of an environmental organization seemed a natural step to him, a view that was shared by the organization's board.

The long hours required to accomplish goals matter less when there is a genuine match between the person and the mission.

Leaders or Managers

It does require vision to lead, to nurture an organization, to accomplish new goals, but leaders also need management skills to assure financial stability and programmatic integrity.

Some experts distinguish between leaders and managers. They feel that leaders are visionaries who see the big picture, while managers concentrate on the day-to-day issues. It does require vision to lead, to nurture an organization, to accomplish new goals, but leaders also need management skills to assure financial stability and programmatic integrity. This is a complex topic where a rigid division does not work neatly.

Heads of nonprofits often fail if they do not have a balance of leadership and management ability. Being able to articulate vision inspires staff and funders. But if working conditions are unsatisfactory because of poor management or programs do not deliver on their promise, staff and donors will become disenchanted. A search committee will want to develop questions to learn if candidates have both leadership and management skills.

Leadership does not have to be confined to one person. Good executive directors encourage the leadership of others. Organizations thrive when managers, as well as staff, demonstrate skills in motivating others and seeing new possibilities to further the mission.

Good leaders know their own strengths and weaknesses and hire people with complementary interests and skills. Leaders who are also good managers know the right questions to ask to assure that work delegated is on target. They are able to spot problems and pay attention to the overall operation which supports the vision. Strong financial management skills are critical for nonprofit leaders.

Paying attention to what really matters

Executive directors can assume there will be more to do than is humanly possible. Successful leaders can sort out what is most important and retain that focus through a myriad of distractions. One way to retain focus is to communicate what they care about and why that matters to the organizational mission. Good leaders knowingly guard their time and energy to focus on the areas which are most important to the success of the organization.

Effective leaders manage strategically.

Effective leaders manage strategically. Their focus is on the mission, vision and goals. Leaders model what really matters by using the mission, and its implied values, as a basis for behavior and decisions. They communicate this frequently, and effectively; everything they do or say reinforces the mission and the goals.

Leaders who focus on the vision also need to depend on solid management skills so they can quickly understand the key issues but not become enmeshed in the details. They know the right questions to ask to assure that all the pieces are working smoothly. Reference interviews will help a search committee understand if the candidates have the ability to focus on the big picture, communicate it in a meaningful way and be "on top" of the work which supports the vision.

Mentoring

True leaders are quick learners and open to new learning. Most candidates will describe one or more mentors, people who served as their role models. Aspiring leaders become students of leadership styles, observing what was effective and what was not. Through the process, they become more conscious of developing their own leadership skills. Because they are self-aware, they adapt what they learn to fit who they are, blending what they learned and what is comfortable for them.

Some people in leadership roles enjoy mentoring others, sharing what they have learned. Effective mentors are able to understand an individual's potential, abilities and learning curve. This quality is linked to having an appreciation for staff contributions and a concern for them as individuals. Leaders who consciously mentor are helping to improve the skills within the organization and within the field. Understanding a candidate's mentors and mentoring will help a search committee know a person more fully.

Understanding a candidate's mentors and mentoring will help a search committee know a person more fully.

Hiring

Hiring well is an important attribute of successful leaders. They know that they need talented and dedicated staff at every level. Leaders who are self-aware will hire staff with complementary abilities. A valuable question for a search committee to ask a candidate is how he or she approached hiring in their organization and to describe when and why there were new hires. Asking in what ways the abilities of staff complement those of the candidate will add more insights both during the interview and in speaking with references.

Recruiting and retaining good staff requires setting a tone for a healthy workplace which provides support and appreciation. Strong leaders retain staff by working to assure equitable salaries, professional development opportunities and evaluation geared to recognition and growth.

Developing a diverse workforce requires a conscious effort on the part of leaders. This can take many forms. A welcoming workplace environment, based on a conscious assessment and appropriate changes is one avenue. Policies which require candidates of color in every search provide a standard and send an important message. Guidance in developing a varied outreach program will assure the diversity of candidates in every search. Diversity among board members and senior administrators illustrates commitment. A search committee will want to thoroughly understand each candidate's success in hiring and retaining staff and his or her commitment and actions to develop a diverse workforce. The committee can begin to learn this in the initial interview, in subsequent ones or from references.

Delegating

Complementing good hiring is the ability to delegate and support the work of staff. Achieving organizational goals requires everyone's best contributions. Talented executive directors hire well to maximize the available talent and then delegate wisely. People who fail to delegate, and become absorbed in details, not only have no time for long-range planning but are not using resources well to achieve organizational goals. Delegating is the way to build staff quality, trust and loyalty. The lack of the ability to delegate is one reason executive directors fail.

Good leaders are adept at balancing support and delegation. They are approachable and supportive so staff want to relate progress and are comfortable explaining problems. A search committee will want to know how a candidate delegates and checks in with both seasoned and new employees. This information will provide good insights into this important skill, so necessary for success.

Letting Employees Go

Having to ask someone to leave is never easy. Often there is a tension between what is best for the program and its clients and the personal situation of the employee. When a search committee interviews candidates, asking about a difficult termination experience and how the candidate worked through it will reveal a great deal about the person's sensitivity, problem-solving skills and decision-making. This is also a good question for references.

Sense of self

Because good leaders understand themselves and are clear about their values, they can make decisions which they feel are right and not take it personally when people disagree. They can also absorb the community's anxiety in times of crisis, remaining calm, visible and reassuring. A search committee will want to know if candidates have the experience, and the strength and wisdom, to guide a community through difficult decisions and times of crisis.

Effective leaders are not afraid of trying something new, taking a risk which could improve programs or services. They can also accept failure and learn from it. Understanding whether a candidate has taken risks and what the outcome was, and whether he or she learned from mistakes, will illustrate more about the leader under consideration. Someone who is comfortable explaining a mistake and what he or she learned from it is most likely self-aware and open to learning and constructive criticism.

Understanding whether a candidate has taken risks and what the outcome was, and whether he or she learned from mistakes, will illustrate more about the leader under consideration.

People with a strong sense of self do not need the limelight. They like working with a team and will share the credit for any successes while taking responsibility for any failures. They are collaborative for all the right reasons — because it advances the work of the nonprofit organization.

Charisma

Often people think of charisma as an essential element of leadership but there are many successful and effective executive directors with quiet personalities who would not be described as charismatic. They are, however, articulate about the mission and why it matters, have foresight in shaping the future and lead organizations that flourish. Thinking about the full range of leadership qualities will help search committees assess how important charisma is to its organization. A community of strong personalities may respond better to a very out-going person, while for another group, that characteristic may not be right.

Search committees often wrestle with this decision, wondering how they could be attracted to very different personalities. One committee, in lengthy discussions about the top two finalists, recognized that the charismatic person would initially help them attract new members but the quieter person was more like them and would be a better fit in the long-term. They chose the quieter person and more than ten years later, she continues to be the right leader for them.

Creativity

Static organizations tend to wither and fade away. Successful organizations are creative, dynamic places which work to improve existing programs and may develop new ones to further their core work. The goal of a search committee is to discover how candidates have influenced the organizations they currently serve.

Knowing that a candidate is adept at developing new ideas is instructive, ,but it is also important to know whether a candidate recognized good ideas created by others and supported their development.

Some leaders are creative and innovative and the primary source of new ideas. Others hire creative and innovative people and support their ideas. Either way, a nonprofit is thriving and growing. Knowing that a candidate is adept at developing new ideas is instructive, but it is also important to know whether a candidate recognized good ideas created by others and supported their development.

These thoughts about leadership can help a search committee better understand the people they interview and the attributes and experience individual candidates would bring. The following chapter explains how to create a description of the organization and its goals which will attract the leaders an organization wants.

Developing the Written Description

The purpose of this chapter is to explain how meeting with constituent groups helps a search committee gather input in order to shape the comprehensive statement which describes the organization and the role of the next executive director.

Introduction

The search committee's interaction with the community is an essential part of the process. It has two benefits. The first is that the dialogues provide a way for the community to become part of the transition as they help to shape future goals and a common vision. The second is that the dialogues with constituents are an important part of the committee's learning experience, providing insights beyond what they have read or heard before.

Before the meetings with the community, each search committee member would review the organization's existing written materials: annual reports, the budget overview, brochures, evaluation materials or other printed information, and the Web page. With this as background, each search committee member is starting with the same information and is then ready to further his or her understanding through community dialogues.

Sharing information about the search process can also reduce the community's anxiety and ensure that there is two-way communication. Each meeting could begin with an introduction of search committee members who are present and an overview of the process and the timeline; this helps to demystify the process. The search committee can also talk about the specific plans for regular communication during the search.

The community dialogues influence the development of the written description in several ways. Through these dialogues common goals emerge and the clarity around goals shapes the way the search committee envisions the experiences and abilities of the next executive director. The description of strengths which the community provides is important for presenting the organization well to those who do not know it. This preparation can have a positive influence on the way outsiders form their first impressions of the organization.

Organizational/community meetings

The search committee will want to meet with every community group in order to have a well-rounded view of the organization, its culture, values, successes, goals and challenges.

The search committee will want to meet with every community group in order to have a well-rounded view of the organization, its culture, values, successes, goals and challenges. While search committee members are already connected to the organization, each person has a unique perspective and most probably does not have the global view which the community input will provide. These meetings will often reveal common themes around values and accomplishments and about issues or goals.

Most likely only a few committee members can take the time to participate in all of the meetings. It is helpful if everyone can attend at least one community meeting to get a flavor of the community's responses.

As a starting point, here is a sample list of constituent groups:

- board,
- current executive director,
- senior administrators,
- program and administrative staff,
- funders, if possible, and
- constituents/clients.

After introducing the search committee members and explaining the overall process, the search committee member who is facilitating the meeting can explain that the organization wants to present its strengths to prospective candidates and for that reason the focus is on the future and not on past problems. He or she can also explain that, for recruiting prospective candidates, a vision of the future is much more appealing than a focus on the past. The facilitator for the committee would describe how the community input will help in developing the description of the organization, its goals and the criteria for the next executive director.

It is important for the search committee to explain what they need from the community meetings and why they need it. A good tactic is to remind people that, while the focus is on future challenges and goals, there is still room to discuss what is not-so-perfect, and that the search process and the community meetings are an opportunity to create a more positive future. In an organization with significant internal tensions, some people will still want to air their grievances. The facilitator may have to work to keep the discussion on the topics so that the meeting does not disintegrate into a gripe session which will not provide the information the committee needs.

People generally enjoy talking about their work and the future, so the questions listed below will easily produce good conversations. The questions are designed to shape the dialogue in a positive way and to give it focus so that the committee learns what it needs.

Four good questions to ask are:

- What are the strengths of the organization?
- What are its challenges/goals?
- How would you describe the ideal experience of the next leader, and
- How would you describe the ideal leadership qualities of the next executive director?

While the meetings provide a forum for the larger community to share their thoughts, they also give committee members a fuller sense of what is working well and what is not. Much of what the community shares will find its way into the description which the search committee creates, and this re-enforces the importance of the community's input.

Using the information

Meeting with constituencies will give search committee members a comprehensive view of their organization and a great deal of material for the written description. The meetings will also provide wonderful stories to share with prospective candidates. This preparation will shape the way the search committee thinks about "ideal" candidates because they will have a clearer sense of the organization's needs and goals.

An organization may have done some of this reflective and goal-setting work prior to the search through an accrediting process or a report for funders or in preparation for an evaluation by funders. There may have been a recent strategic planning process or a new annual report or a feasibility study prior to a capital campaign. This prior work may prepare people to respond more

Meeting with constituencies will give search committee members a comprehensive view of their organization and a great deal of material for the written description.

easily. Focusing now on goals and leadership and seeking input into this process is still critical for building a common vision as a basis for the search. Because the focus now is on the future and future leadership, this is a new topic.

The description of the organization, its goals and the role of the next executive director

Minimizing problems or difficulties may result in more applications but fewer serious or qualified candidates.

After meeting with community groups, the search committee would use the information gathered in the sessions to create a unique description, an accurate portrayal which stresses both the positive aspects as well as the goals. It is important to convey the appealing aspects of the job so that candidates have a clear picture of the positive and exciting parts of the job. At the same time, goals provide a realistic picture of how formidable the challenges are. Minimizing problems or difficulties may result in more applications but fewer serious or qualified candidates.

The written description is an introduction and should have sufficient information to be intriguing. A length of two to four pages is optimal. Other documents can provide more detail for candidates later in the process.

Here is an overview of what a written description should contain:

- introduction/overview/marketing the organization,
- a brief history,
- the strengths of the organization,
- the organization's goals,
- program information,
- organizational structure,
- finances,
- the criteria (required experience for the next executive director),
- desired leadership style or personal qualities, and
- information on how to apply.

The introduction

Because this statement is designed to attract candidates, the description should be compelling.

Because this statement is designed to attract candidates, the description should be compelling. The search committee can describe what makes the organization special, what it does well and who it serves. A brochure or proposal to a funder usually conveys the mission and strengths of the organization well and therefore is a help in writing the search description. The interviews with constituent groups will provide wonderful phrases which can make this description distinct and interesting. Including a glimpse of the future, a topic developed further in the goals section, can also be enticing for candidates. This section can include participation in associations and linkages with other organizations — both provide additional credibility.

Describing history

This section would provide background on the history and development of the organization. Describing growth and development along with prior accomplishments sends the message that positive momentum is part of the history.

The strengths

This section might include the number of people served, results of service, a new building, a completed fund-raising campaign, the successful tenure of the current executive director or highlights about staff. The search committee's meetings with constituents will have gathered insights into the strengths, which will make this section real and unique to the organization.

Goals

The description of goals can be broadly defined rather than overly detailed. Examples of too much detail might be a long list of program goals rather than an overview. An example of a broader goal statement is: "We plan to seek accreditation which will help us make our program even better." Defining "better" will be different for each nonprofit, but each can create a more specific statement about its goals.

Program

This section can include information about programs and program outcomes or successes. It could describe how the programs are innovative or distinctive and might include comments from the constituent meetings praising program elements. There might be a description of the range of clients and client services. If facilities have not been mentioned elsewhere, that information could fit here.

Organizational structure

This section can begin with a description of the board: the number of members, the committees, board terms and length of tenure. There might be information about the current executive director, if appropriate, or simply a statement that the executive director reports to the board. Additional information would include other senior administrative positions, the total number of staff and details of staff qualifications.

Finances

A brief overview would include the annual budget, sources of revenue and categories of expenses. This section might also include information on a prior or planned capital campaign, annual fund-raising event or annual appeal.

Required experience for the next executive director

The experience a search committee requires depends on the nature of the work of the organization and its particular goals at the time. There may be some absolute requirements: certification, field of study or areas of experience. Search committees should discuss how they will distinguish what is a requirement from what is preferred in candidates' experience and training. Too many requirements may greatly limit the possibilities. Flexibility, where possible, could provide excellent people whose background the committee could not visualize at the start of the search. Chapter Seven has examples to illustrate differentiating between minimum requirements and preferences. That chapter is essential to creating this section of the description.

An organization with a particular niche can place too much emphasis on one specific skill and underemphasize the totality of leadership skills required. One example is an arts organization which finds an arts expert extremely appealing and neglects to consider the full range of responsibilities and skills needed to succeed as the executive director. Without the leadership and management skills, the narrow expertise may not be enough to make a successful leader.

It is possible for a successful leader whose experience was gained in one field to become a successful leader in an organization whose focus is completely different. Successful leaders are those whose values and concerns mesh with the work or mission of the organization. These interests may be expressed in volunteer work or other outside activities. The executive director of a non-profit focused on music, for example, went on to successfully lead an environmental group because both organizations depended on their membership and his role was to assure that the members were happy. And, he was a concerned environmentalist.

Another successful environmental and public sector leader, accustomed to large, complex organizations and the politics of dealing with many complicated issues and constituencies, became the successful head of a hospital group. Again, he was dealing with complex issues, financial pressures and many constituencies. A situation like this can create lively and useful search committee dialogues about the organization's real needs and the desirability of remaining open to possibilities which are not apparent as the committee begins its work.

Leadership style or personal qualities

Chapter Ten, "The Attributes of Leadership," will help a committee think about leadership qualities and what those mean in the life of a particular organization. The community meetings and conversations will provide the search committee with interesting phrases to describe the qualities of leadership it seeks. The more those qualities relate to the nature of the organization, the easier it will be for the committee to recognize the qualities in candidates it interviews. One caution is that if a job description is interchangeable with that of other organizations, it is probably not conveying a unique message.

Organizational problems can also influence the way a board or search committee thinks about the person it needs. The immediate problems may make a turnaround person look good, but he or she may not be the right leader for the future either in terms of leadership style or abilities. The chapter on leadership is good preparation for thinking about the difference between management skills which can solve short-term problems and leadership skills which will help the organization reach its longer-term goals, and why it is necessary to want a combination of those skills.

How to apply

This section should include a mailing address and possibly an e-mail address for the person receiving the applications. For purposes of confidentiality, applications would go to the search committee chair rather than to the non-

The chapter on leadership is good preparation for thinking about the difference between management skills which can solve short-term problems and leadership skills which will help the organization reach its longer-term goals, and why it is necessary to want a combination of those skills.

profit. A search committee will want to request the resumes of candidates and usually a cover letter. A committee can choose to be specific about what they would like included in the letter. After a candidate has seen the written description, he or she could be asked to describe their particular interest in the job or how their experience fits the organization's goals. A committee might also require the names and telephone numbers of three or four references. It could decide whether or not to request written references or material about a candidate's current organization at this point. Or, a committee could decide to ask for further information only from those candidates it chooses to interview.

This chapter has discussed the process of gathering information from constituents and the key elements of a written description. The next chapter describes the development of an outreach plan.

Forms of Outreach

This chapter provides an overview of the ways a nonprofit can publicize its search and encourages using multiple strategies to reach a wide audience.

Introduction

The search committee has met with the community, developed a compelling written description and is ready for the next phase of its work. Developing a well-rounded strategy for the outreach is critical for the success of the search; the rest of the process depends on the search committee's ability to attract strong candidates.

Two main tasks are essential to developing a strategy for outreach:

- brainstorming territories and identifying the relevant people, organizations, associations, educational institutions and other useful contacts in each territory, and
- determining the most effective means of reaching multiple audiences through advertising, announcements and networking.

Planning the outreach

Just as planning provided a foundation for the overall search process, planning the outreach can assure a successful outcome for this phase. A plan for outreach which includes many different avenues means that a committee will not find itself "stuck" when one strategy is not fruitful. Having to re-strategize after weeks or months of work can set the process behind. Beginning with a variety of ways to let people know about the search is more likely to yield a strong group of candidates.

At this phase of the search, the goal is to think as broadly as possible. The search committee can brainstorm a list of the obvious places to seek potential candidates. The next step is to think of other, less obvious, places or "territories." What are the allied fields where candidates could have gained transferable skills? If the organization provides child care, for instance, a

A plan for outreach which includes many different avenues means that a committee will not find itself "stuck" when one strategy is not fruitful.

logical place to look would be other child-care agencies. What are the less obvious places? Which large organizations provide child care "in-house?" Are nursery schools a good "territory" to explore? Could graduate schools of education lead to other candidates? What other organizations or resources are there?

Each of these "territories" might produce candidates and each has "observers" who know the field well and could recommend additional sources or candidates. A career path might take someone from a nonprofit organization to a position in a university, association or foundation, and he or she might be interested in moving back into a nonprofit agency.

The Internet is a wonderful resource for researching organizations and identifying people who could help.

In most searches, places which provide training and grant licenses can be a good source of ideas. The universities which grant advanced degrees in the relevant field will often post a listing in the career office and/or on their Web site. Better still is to find the "observers," people who teach and have been there awhile, who could recommend potential candidates. People in national organizations, such as associations or foundations, know which programs and leaders are outstanding. Their regional affiliates, as well as local organizations, can also provide information. The Internet is a wonderful resource for researching organizations and identifying people who could help.

After the first phase of brainstorming, the search committee can look at the results to assess if the plan will reach candidates of color. If not, it can brainstorm ways to assure broader outreach. This might include additional organizations, other colleges and universities, associations and funders. Other resources are special interest sub-groups which are part of large associations or organizations. This might be a women's sub-group or an African-American, Asian or Hispanic sub-group. One of the major purposes of sub-groups is networking, so this could be a fruitful resource. In some fields there may be specific journals, which are an efficient way to reach professionals at leadership levels. A statement about inclusiveness in any advertisement or posting will convey the organization's interest in a diverse group of candidates.

Strategies for getting the word out

Once a search committee has determined a broad list of contacts, the next step in the process is to determine the best means to spread the word to each and all of them. One way is to place advertisements in newspapers and other relevant publications. A well-rounded plan will include announcements to the organization's mailing list. Personal calls by a designated person or member of the search committee can supplement these other forms of outreach.

Developing a diverse pool means devising a strategy for each specific situation. In each of the three forms of outreach, discussed below — advertisements, announcements and networking — the search committee will want to check the plan to assure that it will reach people of color, as well as women, in fields where they are under-represented. There are certainly fields where men are under-represented, such as child care or elementary education, so the outreach would reflect each particular circumstance.

Developing a diverse pool means devising a strategy for each specific situation.

Advertisements

Once the written description is complete, it can be the basis for an advertisement. Like the description, the ad's purpose is to market, to state goals and to describe qualifications — both those that are required and those that are preferred.

The first sentence should state the most compelling reason for wanting to lead the organization. It might be because of the importance of the work or because the organization is on the verge of growth or expansion — whatever is the best feature. The next sentence can describe programs, staff and community.

The last sentence in the paragraph could introduce the major goals. This assures that potential candidates know the challenges and it demonstrates that the organization has done its planning in preparation for the search.

The next paragraph can list the qualifications. It is important for the search committee to be clear about what is required and what is preferred. Being clear about the differences leaves an opening for possibilities the committee cannot envision at the start of the process. Defining the minimum requirements carefully, would not limit the candidates unnecessarily. Requirements and the "preferred category" are discussed more fully in Chapter Seven. When the stated qualifications are clear, a potential candidate can assess his or her match for the job.

The description can be welcoming to all by stating that this is an equal opportunity employer. The final section can state the means for applying.

Writing an ad well also focuses the thinking of the committee. Those clear criteria help when the committee reviews applications. The clarity makes it easier to notify candidates who will not be interviewed because they do not meet the requirements.

The board has most likely given the search committee an overall budget, and the committee would determine a budget for advertising and how to use it most effectively. There are many choices. Regional newspapers are the most obvious, particularly if the organization wants local candidates and can not afford moving costs. Professional journals are another possibility. Association newsletters and their Web sites provide further coverage. Web sites for jobs, particularly nonprofit jobs, are another option for attracting out-of-state candidates. This method is now widely used and often reasonably priced. University placement offices will list jobs, and these are often posted electronically. Organizations which are searching also post the job descriptions on their own Web sites. A brainstorming session within the search committee can develop the range of possibilities that suit the organization and its budget.

Announcements

Announcements are another part of the outreach strategy. Usually these are mailed to as many people as the search committee can think of and can afford to contact through a mailing. This might include any list the organization already uses to rally friends or support or to inform or up-date people. Announcements can be included in a newsletter or another planned mailing to minimize costs.

Specifically for the search, the committee could expand the mailing list by adding the executive directors of other organizations who might recommend candidates or be personally interested. The organization may already have access to such a list or an association might provide one. Association directories contain valuable information about other organizations. Searching the Web for parallel organizations can also be useful. Their sites usually list administrators and contact information.

The announcement can be longer than the ad since it will be mailed. If the written description is no more than two pages, the committee can send that. If the description is longer, the committee can simply excerpt relevant portions. To assure that the announcement reaches diverse communities, it can be sent to community leaders and organizations, including churches and other community resources, particularly if the search is a local one. For a national search, the ideas in the advertising and planning sections will help the committee achieve wide coverage.

The networking plan

While ads and announcements may be productive, it is best not to rely on them completely. Networking is more targeted and personal than the ads or announcements and will reach candidates who are not reading ads but might respond to a telephone call. Since it is hard to predict at the start of the search process where the best candidates are, or how to best connect with them, a committee would want to test every relevant idea including networking.

"Territories" are again the way to begin thinking about broad coverage in networking. The committee can brainstorm a list of "territories" which fit the organization; this is described at the beginning of this chapter. The "networking" calls might parallel some of the areas for ads or announcements, on the theory that a conversation could be more productive. The calls might also lead to new areas. Once there is a list of "territories," the committee can think of related associations, Web sites, funders, and universities or other professional training places for each of these areas.

A good brainstorming session could identify a range of community organizations, including those which serve communities of color. While the committee may already have decided to send an announcement, a personal call is usually more productive. Web sites often list staff and board members; it is useful to have a name when calling. If a committee creates a list of three "territories" and then thinks of associations, Web sites, funders, universities or other professional training places for each area, plus ways to reach under-represented groups, there will be a substantial list of people to begin calling. Having a list of the ideas makes it easy to begin assigning calls to search committee members.

This chapter provided a guide to developing a broad and strategic outreach plan. The following chapter explains how to engage "sources."

Networking

This chapter describes networking, a proactive way of engaging many sources who can help in the search.

Introduction

Chapter Twelve provided a strategy for reaching potential candidates through advertisements and announcements and suggested supplementing those with networking. Actively recruiting candidates offers many advantages and will call on new skills for the designated "recruiter" or search committee members. This chapter is a guide to understanding and using proactive networking successfully.

What are the benefits?

There are several reasons why networking can identify candidates that more passive methods, such as advertisements, will not. A telephone call is more personal and provides an opportunity for dialogue. Some people prefer to be asked and would not respond to an ad. Others may never see the ad because they are not reading them. Often people who are not actively looking for a new position have a feeling that it is time for a change, and therefore respond positively to a call from a search committee member.

Another instance where networking is more effective than advertising is when a nonprofit has major challenges. During a conversation, those issues can be discussed and explained. Often the rumors are not the facts or do not provide up-to-date information. Assuming that the organization knows its problems and is working to solve them, an internal recruiter or search committee member is equipped to answer concerns in a positive way. The dialogue can address the issues and provide a better overview of the strengths of the organization and the progress on problems.

In addition, if an organization wants to assure that the applicants will include strong candidates who are women and people of color, networking offers a better option. Many women or people of color may believe that their chances are slim and therefore might not respond to an ad. A personal conversation may make the difference. An organization can meet its goals of successfully diversifying the organization by making a concerted effort to identify strong candidates of color or candidates from under-represented groups in every search.

Keeping an open mind

An organization may already have one or more individuals in mind for the job. While that may seem like the perfect solution, there are some dangers for the organization. One is that it may decrease the energy and scope of the search. Another is that the choice of an executive director has more credibility if there has been a thorough search. Also, there could be complications with those individuals the organization first identified and, during the waiting period, the search is stalled instead of active.

In one search, the person everyone thought was perfect declined to apply — a decision made after long deliberation. Fortunately, the networking was simultaneously identifying other strong candidates.

When a known candidate does apply, it is difficult to assess his or her strengths without a comparison and contrast with others. Seeing other candidates will provide the perspective the committee needs. In some cases, a comparison with others confirmed the strengths of a known candidate. In other cases, the process of evaluating all candidates brought conclusions no one expected. This may have occurred because the search produced stronger candidates or because the search committee had developed a new view of the goals and a different sense of how effective the organization was in comparison with other groups. A search is a great learning experience, and being open to possibilities will mean stronger decisions.

The network calls

There are some logistics to put in place before beginning the networking calls. First, there is a decision about who will be recruiting. Perhaps it will be one or more members of the search committee, or perhaps it will be a staff person; this depends on availability, interest and talent. The next consideration is a telephone line or lines, preferably dedicated to the search so that it will be available for a large volume of calls. An answering machine or voicemail that requires multiple actions can discourage return calls. Ideally,

An organization may already have one or more individuals in mind for the job. While that may seem like the perfect solution, there are some dangers for the organization.

the system will be "user friendly" for sources and candidates. The person making the calls also needs a daily block of time to work on the search and to be available to make and receive calls.

Before making the first call, the "recruiter" would have the job description at hand and would have made notes about key points. The earlier process of writing and discussing the organizational description is good preparation for knowing what to highlight. A good way to begin is to describe the organization, its goals and the requirements for the role of executive director, combining the "marketing" and the facts. The ad is a good model for conveying important information and being brief. One piece of advice is to begin with an easy call, not the most important one. A little practice helps improve the message and the results.

With an outreach plan, described in Chapter Twelve, there is a list of people to begin calling. The starting point is people who will be sources and can recommend candidates. People are busy, so the recruiter should be efficient in describing the search and the ideal candidate. If people ask additional questions, the recruiter can share that information, but always be respectful of the source's time. When people ask questions and the recruiter does not know the answer, he or she can promise to find the answer and call back. This offers a second opportunity to engage an interested source or potential candidate.

In the initial calls the recruiter will ask people to recommend one or more candidates who "fit," or other sources who could be helpful. If the person is stymied about who to recommend, the recruiter could ask for a contact person at another organization, which the search committee or recruiter already identified, or for someone else who is a good networker or mentor.

When someone recommends a candidate, the recruiter would thank them and then follow up with another question asking what in particular makes that person a good match. In a best-case scenario, this provides further information about the potential candidate and confirms that he or she would be a good fit, and it may provide insights about why the person would be interested. That information will help the recruiter when it is time to call the potential candidate.

If the recommendation of a candidate seems off the mark, this provides a chance to explain the necessary experience more clearly and redirect the source's thinking. Hopefully, this will result in a closer match. A recruiter's time is valuable and follow-up questions will assure that his or her time is spent productively — calling potential candidates with the right qualifications.

Testing territories

When the caller reaches a source who is particularly interested in the search and is helpful, it is a good time to pose the "territories" question. The recruiter can explain the territories generated in the network planning and ask if those seem right and if there are others. Another question to ask is which organizations are considered the best in the field. Another could be to identify mentors who enjoy preparing new leaders. At each phase of the outreach, good questions by the recruiter expand the possibilities.

Exchanging information

Busy people are more likely to recommend candidates in response to a brief conversation than by reading something mailed, faxed or e-mailed. Printed materials are a last resort in discussions with sources. Before giving up on a call, the recruiter can ask for another resource who could help. If it is necessary to send information, following up with another call and a specific question may generate useful information.

When someone wants to see more information and is potentially interested in becoming a candidate, that is a positive event. He or she might be willing to provide a résumé at this time, or may want to see the written information first. Most people will want the description e-mailed, which is simple and quick. A recruiter should keep a list of potential candidates and follow up after they have had time to read the information and/or think about the possibility of becoming candidates. This second conversation would be an opportunity to discuss additional questions or to ask if the person will be applying.

When there is a follow-up conversation, shortly after receiving the application, a formal letter of acknowledgement is not necessary. For candidates who apply through ads or announcements, a letter acknowledging receipt of the information is a courtesy, particularly if there will not be a conversation if the person is clearly not qualified or if there will not be a conversation for awhile, for whatever reason. Many people will respond to ads even when it

Busy people are more likely to recommend candidates in response to a brief conversation than by reading something mailed, faxed or e-mailed.

should be clear that they do not meet the minimum criteria. Searches are very time intensive, so recruiters should reserve their conversations for either finding qualified candidates or talking with qualified candidates.

Assuring a strong and diverse pool of candidates

Assessing progress, at the end of a few days or every week, will keep the search on target.

During the outreach by telephone, a recruiter should periodically assess the progress on identifying a diverse group of strong candidates. Are there positive responses? Are all the "territories" covered? Have the "territories" expanded? Is there a diverse pool? Are there strong candidates who seem really interested? If any of the answers is "no" or "uncertain," it is time to re-strategize and redirect the efforts. Assessing progress, at the end of a few days or every week, will keep the search on target.

Knowing when the networking is done

There may be an externally imposed ending point, or deadline for applications, determined by the search committee or the board. It is usually preferable to have a goal for closing the search, but it is also helpful to have a statement that the search will continue until the search committee and the board have identified and interviewed strong candidates. A statement which says, "The search committee will begin reviewing applications in (list a month)" alerts potential candidates to the timeline but also provides flexibility in case more time is needed.

Later in the search, when the search committee is certain of the closing date for applications, that date should be posted internally, put on the organization's Web site, and on any other Web sites where the position is posted. While a committee wants flexibility initially, it also needs a closing date to assure that candidates do not apply after that date. Some candidates may still be mulling over whether to apply; the committee or recruiter would notify them of the closing date. The integrity of the search process would be compromised if applications were accepted after that time.

The networking is continuing while the ads and announcements are also bringing in candidates. All candidates need to be reviewed; the next steps for those who appear to be qualified are telephone interviews and preliminary references. Ending the networking is safe only when there are candidates who are well matched and who would take the job if offered. The search committee must also be sure that the pool of candidates is diverse before concluding that the outreach or networking is done. It is not always easy to predict the strength of the candidates until the search committee has begun interviewing.

It is better to be conservative about ending the networking because the unexpected often happens. Candidates drop out of searches for any number of reasons, including second thoughts about moving, pressure from a spouse, partner or children, a counter-offer from their current organization, or a better offer elsewhere.

It is better to be conservative about ending the networking because the unexpected often happens.

Telephone interviews and preliminary reference calls can help in assessing how many strong, and interested, candidates there are. Chapter Fifteen describes these pre-screening interviews, which can also help to increase candidates' interest. Those pre-screening interviews and initial references help the search committee assess the strength of the "pool" of candidates, but it is hard to know with certainty until the committee has conducted its interviews. If there are doubts before the interviews begin, it is best to re-strategize and continue the networking.

This chapter provided strategies for finding candidates through "sourcing" or "networking," a proactive complement to ads and announcements. The following chapter explains how to understand the applications.

Reading Résumés

The purpose of this chapter is to provide strategies for reviewing résumés and letters of application based on the criteria which the search committee developed.

Introduction

Learning to decipher applications is a process which requires time and practice. There are several reasons why this activity should begin while the networking continues. One reason is that the search committee may discover new "territories" for identifying candidates during the review process. Or, the committee may realize it needs to describe the organization's strengths and requirements better to find candidates who are a better fit. The process of beginning to review résumés also helps a search committee understand how well the outreach is doing and if it needs new strategies or support.

The following sections explain the logistics of keeping files and corresponding with candidates. This is followed by descriptions of useful techniques for reading and evaluating résumés and cover letters. The goal of that review is to make more sense of the candidate's introductory materials and determine the best candidates, those who seem to most closely fit the organization's requirements.

Logistics

The chair of the search committee should always keep a pristine copy of original applications. Later additions to this file might include letters of reference, results of references by search committee members, degree verification and other correspondence. This will become the master file for each candidate.

Each committee member can mark up or highlight copies of applications as a reminder of what seems important or interesting or needs further exploration. If the committee will be reviewing a lot of résumés, keeping the applicants straight can be a challenge. Inexpensive three-ring notebooks or folders for each candidate are useful.

Ideally, an acknowledgment was sent when an application was received. If not, now is the time to do it. If there has been an initial acknowledgment, an update is only needed if several weeks have passed. This letter can be as simple as letting people know the timeline, either the closing date for applications or when the committee will begin reviewing applications.

After the review of résumés is complete, the committee would respond to those who do not meet the criteria. The letter should thank the applicant for his or her interest and offer a diplomatic "sorry." If it is decided that the applicant will not have an interview, it is better that the person be informed of this immediately, rather than months later at the conclusion of the process. For purposes of confidentiality all correspondence with candidates is sent to their home addresses.

Reading applications

Preparation

It is a good idea for the committee to have a discussion about résumé reading ahead of time so that people are looking for the same things. Then, individual members of the search committee can read the résumés on their own to have time to absorb the information.

It is a good idea for the committee to have a discussion about résumé reading ahead of time so that people are looking for the same things.

The search committee can review, discuss and clarify the criteria so everyone has the same understanding of absolute requirements and those that are preferred. That should be clear in the written description and the ad. Making a grid or simply having a chart of bullet points in the two categories -- required and preferred -- will provide a focus. The grid may ease the reading and ranking of the résumés, which makes it a useful tool as long as it does not stifle conversation or possibilities by its inflexibility.

Sorting by minimum requirements

When people are reading résumés on their own, sorting by minimum requirements is helpful. For instance, if the minimum level of administrative experience is three years, it is easy to determine who fits. Another example of a requirement might be work experience in a diverse, urban setting. Usually that would be easy to determine from a résumé. The minimum requirements would help people do an initial sorting before the search committee meets again.

As the individual search committee members review the applications and sort by minimum requirements, they might place some applicants immediately in a "yes" group because they are clearly qualified and there is no doubt they meet the minimum requirements. Others would go into a "no" group because they clearly do not meet the minimum requirements. Then there will be others who do not fit neatly into either group. The reviewer forms this last group when there are unanswered questions. One example of someone who might fall into this third group is an applicant who has three or more years of experience as an administrator but in a completely different field, which the reviewer is not sure is applicable. Or, there may be areas which are not clear and without further information no judgment can be reached. The end result of this first sorting is three groups: those who clearly qualify, those who clearly do not qualify and those the reader is unsure of.

Studying the applications more deeply

After reviewing all of the applications and putting them into preliminary categories, an individual search committee member could spend more time on the most qualified candidates. He or she could make notes on additional experience which could be beneficial. Experience with organizations in the relevant field, awards, unusual study or pertinent publications are worth noting and exploring at greater depth later. Accomplishments such as new program development or increased revenues give a sense of the scope of the person's current job and his or her achievements.

One way to discover more in a résumé is to understand the person's journey or progress.

One way to discover more in a résumé is to understand the person's journey or progress. Reading the résumé backwards, from education or the first job, is a way to figure out what the career path has been. A number of questions will help. Do the jobs have increasing responsibility? Is there a list, or description, of accomplishments? Are they relevant to this organization's needs? Is there budget authority? Supervisory experience? Board experience? Other experiences that match the criteria? Growth in responsibility and accomplishments? How often does the applicant change jobs?

If the organization is looking for an executive director, how much time will he or she spend in external relations? Does the résumé reveal similar experience which is work-related or gained as a volunteer? Fund-raising experience may be required or simply an added asset. Is there mention of fund-raising or service on a community board where the person would be involved in the planning of campaigns or events?

Volunteer work can complement paid work experience and be an indicator of other interests. Fund-raising knowledge or experience is just as valuable if a candidate gained it as a volunteer. If a candidate is a member of a board, that experience can mean greater awareness of the board's role, structure and tasks. Candidates who have served on boards have a deeper understanding of financial oversight, fund-raising and strategic planning. As committee members study the applications, making notes about additional assets is a useful reminder and a way of further understanding and differentiating among the candidates.

Some résumés are hard to read because there seems to be a gap in the work or the chronology is confusing. This might have a logical explanation or might indicate a problem. Explanations might include further education, the birth of children, an illness in the family or moving to a new geographic area. A reader would note questions that any application raises.

Many short-term jobs naturally raise questions. There may be a reason for one short-term job, but a series of them is a concern. A committee should be open to hearing about one instance if there are solid stays at other jobs. A personal problem such as family illness could be the cause of one short-term job. A staff cutback or funding problems might be another reason. Because a good search process is always a learning experience, keeping an open mind helps. A committee should not rule out a qualified candidate until its questions are answered.

Many short-term jobs naturally raise questions.

When committee members, who are reading on their own, review a résumé from a candidate who meets the basic requirements, the next step is to make a list of positive factors and a list of questions. This exercise of reviewing applications will illustrate how some people provide minimalist résumés and are modest about their accomplishments while others provide lengthy documentation that makes it difficult to sort out exactly what this person did. Making notes helps to sort out the different candidates and prepare for the search committee meeting and discussion, and for any later conversations with the candidates.

Presentation and cover letters

Another level of observation is to assess the presentation. The way candidates present material offers clues to their level of interest and their readiness for the role of executive director. Is the résumé professional looking?

Has it been carefully written? Is it easily readable? Is the spelling correct? If it is a very lengthy résumé, are the additional pages worthwhile? Is it well organized?

The same criteria for a professional presentation apply to letters. How professional is the appearance. Is it well written? Is the length appropriate? Are there spelling errors? Does it explain the person's experience and how it relates to this organization?

While résumés usually present a general overview and may not be rewritten each time a person applies for a new position, cover letters for an executive director's position should be written in response to a specific job.

While résumés usually present a general overview and may not be rewritten each time a person applies for a new position, cover letters for an executive director's position should be written in response to a specific job. Is this cover letter written specifically for this organization or is it a generic one which could be sent anywhere? Is it addressed to the person listed in the ad, usually the chair? Has the candidate made reference to the requirements stated in the ad, the announcement or the job description? Is there evidence that the candidate did some research on the organization? Does the person express an interest in the work or the mission?

Reviewing résumés in a search committee meeting

The goal of this meeting is for the committee to agree on candidates who seem the most qualified, those who meet the stated minimum requirements and whom the search committee wants to learn more about. The first time the search committee reviews applications together, it can begin with a brief review of the criteria to assure that everyone has the same understanding, because the review of applications may have raised questions of interpretation.

It might be most efficient to determine first which candidates do not meet the minimum requirements. The chair could ask committee members for their lists and see where there is agreement. If the committee agrees totally on the list of those who do not meet the minimum qualifications, those candidates do not need further discussion. If, after the discussion, there is still no clear consensus on whether some applicants meet the minimum criteria, those candidates can join the ranks of the middle group where there are unanswered questions.

The category of applications in the middle or "on hold' group could include:

- résumés which are not clear, so the committee has questions before it can make a judgment,

- applicants with experience not anticipated in developing the profile,

- candidates the committee wants to compare against later applicants, or

- applicants to consider after the first candidate interviews.

The next step would be for the chair to ask committee members to share their lists of qualified candidates. If there is a difference of opinion, that would be discussed and if there is still uncertainty, the application in question could temporarily go in the middle category to be considered later. As the committee reviews résumés, it will be evident that different people notice different things, which is one of the benefits of having multiple perspectives. For those candidates whom the committee unanimously determines do meet the criteria, the next discussion could address their additional qualifications, which may correspond to the preferred categories or other interesting areas that the search committee had not anticipated initially.

Key points to cover

Here is a list of key points to note during the committee's discussion. Using it will provide a good basis for the committee dialogue. It could also become a guide or chart for those so inclined. The areas to note are:

- How does the candidate's experience compare to the requirements? For example, three years of administrative experience is required; this candidate has five years of experience. Another example: work experience in a diverse urban environment is required; this candidate has worked in two diverse urban settings.

- What additional assets does the candidate bring from the preferred category or a new area? For example, if fund-raising experience is preferred and this candidate writes about having that experience. Another example: board experience was not listed in a preferred category but this candidate has board experience, which is a plus.

- How similar is the candidate's organization to this organization? How similar are the responsibilities and challenges?

- What is the quality of the presentation of materials and the quality of the contents?

- Are there interesting areas to learn more about?

- What other questions does the committee have?

Assessing how many strong candidates there are

The process of reviewing and ranking candidates is also a real test of how strong the pool of applicants is. If there are only a small number of qualified candidates this is the time to continue or renew efforts to identify additional candidates. A strategy session to intensify the outreach could occur now, if there is time, or at a subsequent meeting. This in-depth review might also have highlighted new areas or territories which might have strong candidates. Search committee members may now realize that there are areas they have not pursued sufficiently.

Stopping the identification of new candidates prematurely can result in weak choices to present to the board. Unfortunately, recognizing that weeks or months later results in a longer delay. Strategizing a renewed outreach and making assignments as soon as possible will continue the flow of the search process within the desired time frame.

This may be the only meeting at which the search committee reviews applications or, more likely, this is one of several review meetings. At a minimum, the committee will meet again to review the results of preliminary telephone interviews (Chapter Fifteen). If there will be additional reviews, the committee could decide to defer action on those candidates who are hard to classify and discuss them later, after all the applications are reviewed. An exception would be if a search committee member has strong feelings about a particular application, believes further investigation is needed, and the rest of the committee agrees to this action.

Next steps

The next steps for those candidates who are qualified will depend on the extent of conversations that have already occurred and when they occurred. The following chapter explains how the preliminary interviews and references bring new information to strengthen the decision-making ability of the search committee.

When the committee has reviewed all the applications, it can send a letter to inform the candidates who do not meet the minimum criteria and will not be interviewed. It is more considerate to let them know at this point and to thank them for their interest. For candidates in the "hold" category, a letter could inform them of when the committee hopes to complete the review of applications, particularly if there has been a long period of time since candidates heard from the committee. Because committee members will be speaking with the qualified candidates, no additional letter is required at this time.

This chapter provided strategies for reviewing and ranking applications. The following chapter describes how the committee can use telephone interviews and preliminary references to learn more before determining which candidates will meet with the search committee.

Preliminary Interviews and References

Well-done preliminary interviews and reference checks will assure that the search committee interviews the best candidates — those who are most qualified and truly interested.

Introduction

To make maximum use of the committee's time in the interview process, it is helpful to do some further work to assure that the candidates are interested, that their résumés are accurate and that their salary expectations are within the organization's range.

By now, the search committee has invested considerable time in a careful reading of the candidates' written applications. To make maximum use of the committee's time in the interview process, it is helpful to do some further work to assure that the candidates are interested, that their résumés are accurate and that their salary expectations are within the organization's range. A few minutes spent gathering information can save the committee from hours of wasted time and possible expenses incurred for travel. The other valuable outcome of these conversations is the opportunity for candidates to connect with someone in the organization and, ideally, to heighten their interest in it.

Telephone interviews

The purpose of the initial telephone conversation is to assure that the candidate is interested, to see if his or her experience is relevant and to determine that there are no immediate concerns about the fit. This work might be assigned to the internal "recruiter" or divided among committee members.

In preparation for the conversations, the interviewer can review the résumé to understand the chronology and to jot down questions. Because of confidentiality, the recruiter should call a candidate at home or send an e-mail introducing himself or herself and asking to set up a good time to talk.

One goal of the telephone interview is to learn how accurately the résumé represents the applicant's experience. The best way to do that is to engage the candidate in dialogue. One helpful way to understand the applicant's career is to begin with the first job and learn the motivation for each move and the connections or stories behind each.

As the candidate talks about his or her work, the interviewer will gain a better understanding of the résumé and the person. Details about each job will add to the information about the candidate. Questions could include the size/budget of the agency, its leadership history, successes and challenges. This conversation will illustrate how similar the organizations and jobs are and how much leadership and management experience the applicant has. The interviewer will want to be certain that the résumé is accurate — for example, that the person is still employed if that is what the résumé implies.

At times, this initial interview will reveal issues. These might include inaccuracies in dates of employment, a negative attitude towards former employers or no knowledge of the hiring organization at all. Most people will research an organization prior to submitting an application, which demonstrates interest and initiative. Others simply respond to any advertisement and may be surprised by the call. At the level of executive director, a serious applicant should be willing to invest time to learn more before applying.

Salary discussions

Many ads do not include specific salary information but instead say " salary commensurate with experience." During a telephone conversation the interviewer can ask what the candidate's current salary is and then share the salary range that the organization has set. A search committee would not want to interview a candidate, and incur travel costs, if the person is making considerably more than this nonprofit can afford. On the other hand, if initial discussions with potential candidates reveal that the stated salary range is lower than qualified candidates are already making, the search committee would inform the board, which would need to re-think the issue.

Preliminary reference checks

Many candidates include the names and telephone numbers of references in their applications. During the telephone interview the connection to the references will become clear or the interviewer can ask about them. Work-related references are essential. If the candidate did not provide references, he or she may have some names to offer at this time. The "Confidentiality" and "The Timing of References" sections, in Chapter Nineteen, provide a further explanation and suggestions for initial references. That chapter also contains examples of the kinds of questions which are most helpful. If the search committee has out-of-state candidates, preliminary references help to use resources wisely.

This initial telephone interview can provide a much better sense of the applicant, his or her career path, motivation and level of interest. The preliminary references can corroborate the impression from the telephone interview or raise questions. When the search committee has heard the results of all the telephone interviews and references, it can select the best applicants to continue in the process — those who are most interested and most qualified. This preliminary work assures that the committee's time is well spent. It can be painful to sit through an interview and discover the candidate's résumé did not present him or her accurately, when a telephone call would probably have uncovered this. The telephone conversation is also an opportunity for candidates to make a connection with someone in the organization, to ask questions and to be able to judge better how interested they are.

It can be painful to sit through an interview and discover the candidate's résumé did not present him or her accurately, when a telephone call would probably have uncovered this.

One-on-one interviews

After the initial telephone screening there can be added benefits if there is an opportunity for a representative of the organization to meet with potential candidates in person. A one-on-one discussion provides an opportunity to market the organization's strengths and potential as well as to learn more about the candidate. Cultural differences or questions which may be awkward in a committee interview can be more easily discussed here.

This interview can be more in-depth than the telephone interview but still an informal conversation. The candidate may feel more comfortable asking questions about the last person who held the job, the stability and prospects of the organization, the climate within the nonprofit, as well as any concerns he or she may have about personal or family issues. The interviewer will learn more about the candidate's experience and abilities and what attracts him or her to the position. This interview is feasible if candidates are local or if there is a national conference which fits within the search time frame. Because the committee wants to be equitable, these interviews should be held with all of the qualified candidates because interviewers usually feel more strongly about candidates after meeting with them.

Strong candidates will have other choices; the hiring organization has to market itself to be competitive.

The interviewer has a general understanding of the applicant's background and a sense that this is someone the search committee may want to see. The goal of this face-to-face conversation is to make a personal connection, to answer questions and to heighten the candidate's interest by describing in more detail the strengths and potential of the organization. Strong candidates will have other choices; the hiring organization has to market itself to be competitive.

Ideally, by the time this one-on-one interview takes place, the search committee has formulated the questions it will ask. The interviewer can pursue other areas to add information to the total view of the candidate. If it is not feasible to have one-on-one interviews with all candidates, the telephone interviews can be more comprehensive — incorporating some of the ideas from this section.

A one-on-one interview can also bridge cultural differences. A candidate, or the interviewer, can raise and discuss issues more easily in this less formal discussion than in a group setting. When it is appropriate, that information can be shared with the search committee before the interview, so it does not get in the way.

A one-on-one interview can also bridge cultural differences.

If a candidate is overly modest because of upbringing or cultural norms, a skilled interviewer can discover the challenges and accomplishments not spelled out on the résumé. That information can be shared with the committee. In this more informal interview setting, the interviewer can also explain what facts, in the candidate's experience, are important to the search committee because of the organization's goals. This can encourage an overly modest candidate to share more information.

In one-on-one interviews, applicants may raise issues which can be critical to their continuing in the process. These might include questions about the committee's (and the organization's) readiness to be led by a woman, a person of color or a person who is gay. This informal setting is the chance to answer questions and to encourage the candidacies of strong potential leaders from diverse backgrounds. A personal interview or a comprehensive telephone conversation forms a connection for the candidate which can help maintain his or her interest.

Telephone interviews and preliminary references bring additional information to the search committee, so that it can use its time most effectively by interviewing the most qualified and interested candidates. The following chapter describes the search committee interviews.

Search Committee Interviews

This chapter is an overview of the interview process, including planning and logistics, developing good questions and knowing which problems to avoid.

Introduction

Interviews are the search committee's opportunity to finally meet the applicants and begin to see the results of their work. Search committees are usually nervous before the first interviews and recognize afterwards that the interviews went smoothly because of their preparation.

There are at least two goals for the interview process. After an ideal interview, the search committee will have a better sense of the candidate's experience, more interest in the person and more questions to pursue. Conversely, the candidate will know more about the nonprofit through the committee, be more interested in the position and have additional questions.

The opposite situation can also occur when a committee decides that the person is not right for the organization or the person is not interested in continuing the process. Hopefully, this situation is rare because of the preliminary telephone interviews and references.

Selecting the candidates to interview

After the preliminary interviews and reference checks are complete, the search committee would have a meeting to hear the results. One format for the reports could combine both factual and more personal information. Details about the applicant's current position and other relevant jobs could include: size of the organization, budget, number of employees, number of clients served and major challenges. Information about the organizational structure will illustrate the scope of the candidate's responsibilities. The applicant's current salary is pertinent to be sure that it falls within the range of possibility for this organization. The committee would also want to hear about each candidate's level of interest.

More personal information could include the applicant's reasons for moving to the current job, any stories about bosses or clients which came up in conversations, and other details which explain more about the candidate and his or her experience. While it is illegal to question a candidate about his or her marital status or sexual preference, a candidate will often want to talk about it at this stage. Someone may want to know about opportunities for a spouse to find employment in the area, about good schools for their children or about housing costs. In the case of sexual preference, candidates may want to test the water before committing significant effort to this job possibility.

The committee now has a greater level of information for determining which candidates seem to be the best match. After the discussion, the committee can vote on those candidates it chooses to interview. Again, there may be candidates the committee decides to put in a hold category. This might be because it first wants to interview local candidates or candidates who appear to be stronger.

The recruiter or committee member who has had the most contact with a candidate would call and invite him or her to come for an interview, or alternatively, the chair could decide to do that. Every call is an opportunity to continue to build rapport. The interview time and place would be confirmed in a letter which includes directions and a list of search committee members and their connection to the organization. At this time it would be useful to provide additional information beyond the description/criteria statement. This might include program materials, an annual report or something similar. Detailed budget information, evaluation or accreditation reports are usually part of the package sent later to the finalists, although there may be reasons why it makes sense to send more at this time. Candidates may request additional information at this point.

Reassessing the number of strong candidates

The process of choosing candidates to interview enables the search committee to understand more fully the "ideal" candidates. In order to recommend three or four finalists to the board, the search committee would ideally interview a minimum of eight to ten qualified candidates. If the preliminary interviews and references diminished the committee's interest in some candidates, the committee's discussion could once again assess whether there

In order to recommend three or four finalists to the board, the search committee would ideally interview a minimum of eight to ten qualified candidates.

are a sufficient number of strong candidates, a minimum of eight to ten. If there is doubt, the options are to continue networking and/or to look further at candidates in the "hold" category. Having had these review discussions, the committee members will be more knowledgeable about what to look for in the applications of the middle group and which questions are most important in preliminary telephone interviews and references.

If there is a decision to continue networking, the committee's experience in evaluating candidates and what they have learned about where strong candidates have come from will help to re-energize the outreach. The committee could schedule interviews with the applicants they have selected while continuing to identify additional candidates. They would inform the people interviewed that the committee expects to conduct additional interviews in the next few weeks; this provides a sense of the time line for candidates.

Planning the search committee interviews

For a hard-working committee, this is the exciting time when the preliminary work results in live interviews. There are some logistical aspects to assure that the interview process runs smoothly. Because this is still the confidential phase of the search, the meeting place needs to be one which assures that the candidates will not meet other community members or other candidates. If the committee interviews on weekends, the organization's space may be fine. Or, a search committee member might have a conference room available. Other options are to conduct the interviews in someone's home or at an airport hotel. The kind of space depends on the circumstances – whether there will be out-of-state candidates, budget constraints and the preference of the group. The more informal the organization, the more informal they will want the space to be.

In a group interview by the search committee, the questions should be structured to assure that each candidate has the opportunity to answer the same set of questions and the search committee can compare and contrast candidates based on the same information. If committee members were to interview in small groups, they would not be comparing the same information. People sometimes wonder if the group interview is intimidating. Applicants may vary in how easily they address large groups, but the leader of any nonprofit will face that challenge. The interview with the search committee will reveal this aspect of a candidate's ability.

The committee needs to always be aware that interviews are a way of evaluating each candidate. At the same time, each candidate is evaluating the search committee and, through it, the organization. So the search committee will want to demonstrate its belief in the agency and its work and to show interest in and consideration for each candidate. This includes a close reading of the applicant's résumé and cover letter combined with questions which relate to this organization's goals and the applicant's experience. A review of Chapter Seven will assure that questions are consistent for all candidates and that they are always ethically and legally correct.

The following is an example of an interview format that has worked well. The chair welcomes the candidate, notes the time allotted for the interview, and explains that the committee will ask questions and provide time for the candidate to ask questions as well. Next, each of the search committee members can briefly introduce himself or herself and explain his or her connection to the organization.

The chair can then ask the candidate to present a brief overview (three to five minutes) of his or her career and how their experience might benefit this organization. The committee members have an opportunity to see what a candidate thinks is most important to share. The presentation will be followed by questions from the committee.

The interview questions can be divided among members, which gives the candidate a chance to hear from everyone on the committee. At the end of the interview, the chair would thank the candidate and explain when he or she would next hear from the committee. A chair may be comfortable offering to answer additional questions if the candidate would like to call.

An hour and fifteen minutes, or an hour and a half, is a reasonable amount of time for each candidate, with a break afterwards for the committee to debrief. This summarizing time is also useful for keeping candidates from meeting each other.

The grid which was used in reviewing applications could be helpful again with additional sections for thoughts on leadership style or other new information from the interview. Each person will probably want to keep his or her own notes to refer to during later discussions. Some people like to jot notes on the copy of the résumé. Some committees prepare question sheets with room for note-taking. The best note-taking during an interview is mini-

> The committee needs to always be aware that interviews are a way of evaluating each candidate. At the same time, each candidate is evaluating the search committee and, through it, the organization.

mal, sufficient to remember important points but not so elaborate that people are focusing on their papers rather than the candidates.

Developing Questions

A general rule of thumb is to have a question about each of the goals.

Formulating the job description prepares the search committee for its interviews and questions. The questions should help the search committee understand each candidate's choice of work places, responsibilities, learning and growth — in general, and then in areas of specific interest to the organization, those areas that relate to the goals. A general rule of thumb is to have a question about each of the goals.

Open-ended questions can provide a clearer sense of each candidate. Examples are:

- Describe your organization and major challenges it faces or has faced.

- What is the most difficult decision you have had to make and tell us what you learned from it?

- Describe for us how your prior experience fits our needs. (This will illustrate how much attention he or she has invested in knowing this organization and its priorities.)

In creating questions, a committee would want to explore what a person did, but as important is why the person chose that course. How did the candidate determine the priorities? How would he or she assess the outcome? How was the institution affected? This approach illustrates how a candidate thought as well as how he or she acted.

As a search committee develops open-ended questions, they will want to frame some questions to discover a candidate's ability to think in "big picture" terms. If a committee asks too many detail-oriented questions, they will hear details without knowing how the candidate thinks about the impact of small actions on the broader institution.

A generic set of questions may produce a lot of talk but less real or relevant information.

The examples provided here can stimulate the committee to develop its own questions to fit its specific circumstances. The document which the search committee created for the search has the list of goals which will lead to specific open-ended questions. It takes only minutes to brainstorm a list of good questions. A generic set of questions may produce a lot of talk but less real or relevant information.

In some areas there will not be an exact match of experience, but a little thought will help generate good questions which help the committee learn about a candidate's skills. If a goal is to heighten awareness of the organization and its work, what experiences, qualities or skills seem meaningful? For a young agency that wants to develop to the next stage of maturity, what are the questions which will bring forth skills, abilities and interest in developing an organization? If a goal of the hiring organization is to expand to other cities, does the candidate have any relevant experience? If a goal is to unify existing branches or develop relationships with other organizations, what similar experience does the candidate have or what skills has he or she demonstrated which would be helpful?

These interviews have dual purposes, which are equally important for the search committee to keep in mind. The first purpose is to learn specific information about an applicant's experience, skills and abilities and to begin to assess his or her "fit" with the mission, vision and people of this organization. A second desired outcome is to heighten the candidate's interest in the leadership role. Courtesy, respect, friendliness and appropriate questions will influence how a candidate views the nonprofit and its search committee.

Problems to avoid in interviews

Open-ended questions allow the committee to sit back and listen to candidates and develop a better picture of who they are. Questions which only require a yes or no answer do not provide the same sense of a person. Examples of the latter type of question are:

- Do you get along well with people?
- Do you like fund-raising?
- Are you a team player?

Because these questions only require a one word answer, the search committee may not learn much about the candidates. And it would be surprising if a candidate said he or she did not get along well with people or answered "no" to those other generic questions.

The search committee has invited those candidates whose experience seems most relevant; at this point they seem to be the best matches. During the interview, the questions should be positive, focusing on learning more about that experience. Questions should not imply that a candidate is deficient in

Open-ended questions allow the committee to sit back and listen to candidates and develop a better picture of who they are.

some area, because the committee has already determined that he or she meets the minimum criteria. If, for instance, fund-raising is a "preferred" area, questions should be aimed at discovering what a candidate has observed or learned about it and how he or she would learn more. If fund-raising was not a minimum criterion, the search committee would not want to criticize a candidate's lack of that experience. That may seem self-evident, but since it has happened, a reminder here is useful.

Questions in the "what if" category test the person's ability to think quickly, to interview well and to guess at what the committee wants to hear.

Another type of question which should be avoided is the "what if" question." Questions in the "what if" category test the person's ability to think quickly, to interview well and to guess at what the committee wants to hear. An example is: "What if you become our executive director? How would you solve our financial problems?" The "what if" questions may not reveal an applicant's experience, method of approaching problems, successes, failures or learning. The candidate may say that he or she will do exactly what he or she believes the committee wants to hear, and there is nothing in the response to "what if" questions that a committee can check with references. More information could be gained by asking, "Has your organization had financial problems and how have you dealt with them?" That information can be confirmed through discussions with references.

Unfortunately, if a committee only asks "what if" questions, the interview has not provided further information about how well this person has dealt with prior challenges and what he or she has learned from them. That specific information is real data which the search committee needs.

When to reserve judgment

Reserving judgment, while seeking more information, will assure that the committee makes informed decisions.

In this phase of the search, the committee is learning a great deal but there is still much more to learn. Reserving judgment, while seeking more information, will assure that the committee makes informed decisions. There are a number of situations where more information would help the search committee in its decision-making.

One example is if the search committee is impressed with a candidate but suspects that he or she is simply saying what the committee wants to hear because his or her answers sound too good to be true. References and a visit to a candidate's workplace may ease those concerns or validate them. Either way, it is worth knowing.

One search committee dismissed a positive interview as just the performance of a good politician, because ten years earlier the candidate had a leadership role in a state agency where they suspected she had developed political skills. After references and a visit to her current organization, the committee discovered that the candidate's words truly reflected her beliefs and actions. Ultimately, the board hired her and she successfully leads that nonprofit a decade later.

In another case, an applicant impressed a committee during an interview by answering every question as if he were "already one of us," but the committee was concerned that the candidate was more introverted than the gregarious current executive director. However, a check of references dispelled concerns about the candidate's leadership ability, and a visit to his workplace made an even stronger impression. While members of the search committee planned to ask the questions and do the evaluating, they were peppered by questions from staff and constituents about whether the visiting organization was good enough for their boss.

There are several reasons to continue investigating a candidate the committee is unsure about. It is possible to grade an interview as a "B" or "C" and have an "A" candidate. It could be that the applicant has not interviewed often and is nervous, or that he or she had been taught that speaking of one's accomplishments is not polite. A committee also needs to consider if cultural differences might be a factor. If there are reasonable doubts, the best option is to gather more information before dismissing someone based on one interview.

Here is another example of an awkward interview which left the committee uncertain. The candidate sat stiffly and did not make eye contact but was impressive enough in his answers that the committee wanted to know more, including why he seemed aloof. It turned out that the candidate had the flu and was controlling his nausea by keeping his head motionless and staring at his papers. After learning this, the search committee decided to call references. Fifteen years later that candidate is still the successful executive director of the same organization.

Other cautionary notes

At the other extreme, there are times when a committee is so impressed by an interview that they want to take a vote immediately and bypass discussion. If that happens, valuable insights and viewpoints are left unvoiced. Committee members should remember that, while this interview is an important step in the process and it may feel as if a decision could be based on it, the interview is only one part of the information-gathering process. Without thorough references, a committee really only has an impression and not the facts it needs. The search will be better served by sticking to the process. And candidates do change their minds and decide not to leave their current position or opt for a job elsewhere, a practical reason for not relying on one candidate.

Ideally, the committee will complete its interviews and have a number of candidates they like — without ranking them. The recommendations of the search committee to the board are important to the future of the organization and deserve a thoughtful, reasoned process derived from as much information as possible. The topic of recommendations of unranked candidates is introduced in Chapter Three.

Debriefing after each interview

Debriefing after each interview is an opportunity to hear different views, to learn from what others observed, and to develop an even clearer sense of what the organization needs and what the possibilities are.

Debriefing after each interview is an opportunity to hear different views, to learn from what others observed, and to develop an even clearer sense of what the organization needs and what the possibilities are. The chair can set up a pattern so that each search committee member speaks in turn. A useful format is to ask each member to comment first on the strengths he or she noted, and when everyone has done that, ask each to raise concerns and questions. This keeps the dialogue open and each person is contributing his or her perspective, building a stronger total view.

After a day or weekend of interviewing, the committee may want to have a discussion to summarize which candidates it believes are the strongest based on the interviews. In the discussion, committee members can refer to their notes to support their thoughts. While grids may be useful for taking notes, their use in rating candidates can stifle meaningful dialogue about the organization's goals and candidates' experience and abilities.

In some cases, there may be candidates whom the committee decides should not be considered further. The reasons might be negativity towards current or past employers, indiscretion in divulging information which should be confidential, or simply that the person did not seem to have sufficient experience or the ability to respond well to the questions. One would hope that the preliminary telephone interviews and references would have discovered this, but they may not have.

This chapter provided an overview of the interview process. The following chapter describes the process for selecting finalists when the interviews are complete.

Selecting the Finalists

*This chapter is designed to help the
search committee evaluate the strength
of the candidate group before selecting
finalists, and then describes a process
for that selection.*

Introduction

After the search committee has interviewed those candidates it considered
most qualified, it will want to evaluate the results. The goal is to hire an
executive director who will be successful long-term. Therefore the committee needs to feel confident about the qualifications of the candidates it recommends to the board and that the number of finalists will assure that the
board has real choices. A thoughtful process will assure that happens.

There are several stages to the process of determining whether or not the
committee is ready to pick finalists and, if it is, conduct careful discussions
to select the strongest finalists. The section on "Evaluating the results to
this point" will help the search committee decide if it has a sufficient number of strong candidates or if more outreach is necessary.

Preparing for the meeting

To prepare for the meeting, search committee members should review the
following information:

- the criteria statement and the chart derived from it,
- the candidates' files,
- individual notes from the committee interviews, and
- preliminary references.

Two new items need to be completed before the committee meets to evaluate the candidates:

- an overview of applications, and
- updated candidate information.

Prior to the meeting, a member of the committee can create an overview of applications, including the number of applications, number of qualified candidates, number of people interviewed and gender and ethnic diversity information. This will be valuable as the committee evaluates its readiness to select finalists and will be useful information to present later to the board and to the community.

Since some amount of time has most likely elapsed after the interviews, it would be wise to check in with candidates before the next search committee meeting to assure that each is still interested. If there are doubts about a candidate's interest or salary expectations, this is the time to explore them — prior to the meeting so that the committee has current information on the people it is evaluating.

The chair can call each candidate and explain that the committee will be meeting to select finalists and the purpose of the call is to update information. The questions to pursue are: if he or she is still interested, if there are competing deadlines, if there are other issues or concerns, and if there are any remaining salary issues. These dialogues have two benefits. They further the connection with potential finalists and they bring information to the committee so they can assess how many strong candidates they have who are really interested in the organization.

The preliminary references would support (or refute) impressions from the interviews with the search committee. These references would supplement observations from the interviews and the chair's telephone discussions. If the candidate did not want the committee to check references until a later point, this is that point. While individuals may want to reserve some references until after becoming an official finalist, there are certainly a number of references the candidate could have the committee contact at this stage. The committee needs the preliminary references prior to its meeting. It would be embarrassing for an organization to announce finalists and then discover major flaws or inaccuracies in its understanding of a candidate's experience.

Evaluating the results to this point

With up-to-date information on candidates' interest, the committee is ready to evaluate its choices. The first goal is to determine if there are a sufficient number of strong candidates who would take the position if it were offered. After the interviews, the committee has more information to support its

Since some amount of time has most likely elapsed after the interviews, it would be wise to check in with candidates before the next search committee meeting to assure that each is still interested.

If the candidate did not want the committee to check references until a later point, this is that point.

evaluation of candidates to see if they meet the following criteria:

- sufficient experience,
- successful experience and a career path with progressively more responsibility,
- preliminary references which are positive and suggest competence in the required areas as well as leadership skills,
- salary expectations the organization can meet, and
- a strong interest in continuing in the process.

While "chemistry" between a candidate and the search committee is always a factor, it is not a sufficient reason to select someone as a finalist.

There are a few areas where the committee needs to be cautious. While "chemistry" between a candidate and the search committee is always a factor, it is not a sufficient reason to select someone as a finalist. "Chemistry" has to be accompanied by other definable attributes and significant, successful experience. A solid discussion of how well the candidates meet the criteria and what the reference interviews reveal should help a committee move beyond "chemistry" to facts.

There are other "tests" of the committee's readiness to pick finalists and end the networking process. The overview of applications will illustrate how well the committee met its goals for diversity. The committee should assess if there is diversity both in gender and ethnicity. If this was a priority during the search, the end result hopefully reflects that effort. A lack of diversity could affect how the community views the work of the search committee.

Another "test" would be to assess whether or not there are candidates who illustrate the committee's broad and creative view of the possibilities for the future. Ideally, the committee's message and networking resulted in exciting candidates capable of helping the organization achieve its goals. Naturally, the committee wants to be proud of its work and feel positive and secure in its recommendations to the board. Settling for candidates who do not seem to have the potential the organization envisioned would undermine the potential opportunities which the search offers.

Picking finalists means that no additional applications will be accepted and the networking and outreach phases end.

Picking finalists means that no additional applications will be accepted and the networking and outreach phases end. If the search committee is uncertain about whether there are a sufficient number of strong candidates, it will need to continue searching and delay naming finalists. While this is never a pleasant thought, the choice of the right executive director is a major decision and worth taking the necessary time now. The good news is that if a committee does need to continue searching, it now has a much better sense of where to look most productively as it makes a concerted effort to identify additional candidates. The chapter on networking will also be helpful in re-strategizing.

A few extra weeks at this point are preferable to a perception that the search process had weak results or a situation where the organization settles for an executive director who turns out to be a mistake. That situation would be very disappointing as well as costly.

Continuing the dialogue when there is a strong group of candidates

In the best-case scenario there are a number of viable candidates, so the committee's work now is to recommend unranked finalists to the board. Revisiting the criteria statement and the organizational goals is a good beginning for the discussion. The grid, used for evaluating applications, can be a helpful way to encourage dialogue about the strengths each candidate would bring. It is a useful reminder of the key points, a basis for discussion, but not a substitute for it.

This phase of the discussion would include:

- each candidate's strengths in the required experience areas,
- the additional assets each would bring,
- where each candidate would need to grow,
- other insights from the preliminary references, and
- the key organizational goals and the capacity of each candidate to help achieve them.

Hearing from each committee member, in turn, assures that each has the opportunity to contribute observations and thoughts, and the committee as a whole has the benefit of the collective insights.

For most committees, the conclusions will emerge easily from the discussion. For others, a more structured approach may be more comfortable. During the meeting, the committee could jointly develop a chart for each person outlining the key points listed above. One person can serve as recorder, with everyone contributing. It may be tempting for one committee member to

A few extra weeks at this point are preferable to a perception that the search process had weak results or a situation where the organization settles for an executive director who turns out to be a mistake.

offer to create the chart, but that stops discussion and becomes one person's view.

After a thorough discussion of candidates, the committee can see if its initial sense of the number of strong candidates remains the same. While the committee began this meeting with a preliminary assessment of whether it was ready to select finalists, this would be a logical time to reassess that decision to assure that there are still a sufficient number of strong candidates. Ideally, when the committee completes its work there are at least three or four strong finalists. The board and the organization expect and deserve good choices. Assuming that the committee is comfortable with the finalists it has selected, it is ready to move forward.

While the committee began this meeting with a preliminary assessment of whether it was ready to select finalists, this would be a logical time to reassess that decision to assure that there are still a sufficient number of strong candidates.

There is one other decision some committees might choose to make. If there is a terrific candidate, whom the committee wants to invite to be a finalist but is not sure that he or she will accept, the committee can decide if it wants to select a larger number of finalists. For example, if the committee has selected three people, it could decide if there is a fourth candidate who would be acceptable if one of the three declines. Deciding this in committee gives the person who will do the calling the flexibility he or she might need without the necessity of an additional meeting. Often, those candidates under consideration are reasonably close to each other in terms of their experience and leadership ability -- at least as far as the committee knows at this point.

After the committee has selected finalists, the chair, or another familiar, friendly search committee member can make the call to begin the scheduling process. There is information in the next chapter on the logistics of those visits. The chair of the search committee would also call and thank those candidates who were interviewed by the search committee but who will not be invited back as finalists. A formal letter can follow that conversation.

The search committee would then prepare information for the board and the community. The board would receive all of the written material presented by the finalists and the committee's overview explaining why it recommended these individuals. The format of this overview could follow the five points of the discussion outline above, with added thoughts from the committee's insights. The overview of applications, including gender and ethnic diversity, would also be useful for the board to see. Communication to the community could include the overview and the "bios" of the finalists described in the next chapter.

Through this thorough discussion, a search committee continues its learning process as it evaluates the information it has up to this point. The committee would summarize the work it has completed to support the board's learning process. Because there are other steps in the search process there is still much more to learn and therefore the search committee recommends finalists to the board without ranking them. With unranked finalists the board will invest fully in learning all they can about each person in order to select the best candidate.

The learning process continues

At this point, the search committee has contributed its best judgment based on the evidence it now has. The remainder of the process will build on the foundation the committee has provided. Important additional information will come from the finalists' visits to the organization and the comprehensive references. Presenting finalists without ranking assures that the learning process continues without bias and that the board will make its decision based on the total of accumulated information.

Selecting finalists is a big step, and an exciting one. The purpose of selecting finalists is to choose the best candidates given the information available at this point and then to continue learning more. Seeing how the finalists interact with members of the community and seeing the kinds of questions they ask will provide more insights into personalities and interests. Because the finalists' visits encompass a day or more, the search committee and the board have the opportunity to see candidates at greater length, in different settings. These observations can confirm mutual interest, but in other cases a candidate will not wear well during the longer visit or will withdraw from the process. This is the reason for being certain that there is enough strength and interest among the finalists to assure that the board will have real and credible choices. Obviously having only two finalists is more of a risk; three or four strong finalists are preferable.

The weeks ahead will bring new data and could bring unexpected surprises as well. Here is one example. In an interview with the board, a finalist was vague and unfocused, which was totally unlike the strong initial interview with the search committee. The reason turned out to be a spouse who had announced that morning, "You can move if you want, but I'm not going." The candidate limped through the rest of the visit and then withdrew from

Presenting finalists without ranking assures that the learning process continues without bias and that the board will make its decision based on the total of accumulated information.

the search. This situation illustrates how interviews are one piece of information gathering but rarely tell the whole story. Having multiple, unranked finalists allows time for the rest of the process and learning to unfold.

Much more information is readily available and critical to the board's ultimate decision. If everyone keeps an open mind about learning more, the result will be a stronger decision. Thorough references will let the board learn how people who have worked with the candidate evaluate his or her performance. People to whom the candidate reports and people who work for him or her add other important perspectives. That information, coupled with the finalists' visits, adds to the growing and more detailed picture of each finalist.

This chapter has provided a process for evaluating whether or not the committee is ready to select finalists or needs to intensify the outreach, as well as a process for selecting finalists when the committee determines that it is ready. The next chapter explains how to plan the visits to the community.

Finalists

The finalists' visits serve three purposes: including the community in the search process again, providing the finalists with an in-depth view of the organization and having an opportunity to learn more about them.

Introduction

Finalists are candidates who have moved successfully through the process: the initial application, one or more interviews, preliminary references and an invitation to meet the staff and community. At this point, the community wants the opportunity to meet the finalists and finalists also want to learn more about the organization. This chapter explains how to plan so that the community and the candidates and their families have their needs met.

At this point, the community wants the opportunity to meet the finalists and finalists also want to learn more about the organization.

The plan for the finalists' visits would include:

- discussing board opportunities/obligations during the visits,
- encouraging open minds as information is gathered,
- communicating with the community,
- preparing brief descriptions of the finalists,
- sending additional information to the finalists,
- developing the schedule for each person,
- making plans for family members,
- preparing the "impressions" form,
- determining how to maximize the visits,
- deciding if it is possible and/or desirable to visit the finalists' organizations, and
- assigning reference calls.

The board's role during the visits

The search committee has successfully brought the process to this point. It will continue to be helpful during the visits of the finalists, but this is a time

The board's selection of the next executive director is most likely the most important decision it will make.

which requires the board's full attention. The board's selection of the next executive director is most likely the most important decision it will make. Therefore, creating the schedule for finalists has to take into consideration the best times for meetings to assure that the full board can be present.

In addition, it would be valuable to have individual board members observe the finalists in settings other than the formal board sessions. These occasions might include sitting in, where appropriate, in a meeting with staff, constituents, funders or community leaders. Or, they could have a meal with the finalist, give a tour of the facility or the area, be present at a meeting concerning compensation and contract, attend the wrap-up meeting or something else the board devises. The observations of board members from these additional perspectives will provide more valuable information and a well-rounded view of each finalist. It will also provide perspective on the impressions which constituents share.

The preparation of information about finalists

A simple two paragraph "bio," or biography, of each candidate is a good introduction for staff. This bio would include job history, education and experience which relates to the organization's published goals. Only with the permission of the candidate can the full application package be available to everyone. That file is usually placed in the front office. The search committee will share more extensive information with the board, for example: the complete file with letters, résumé and other materials such as writing samples and information brochures about his or her current workplace. Information for finalists, discussed later in this chapter, would be sent to them before their visit.

Being open to the next phase of learning

At this point in the search
process, board members
often begin to identify their
favorite candidates. Since
this would be based on
incomplete information, it
would be wise to resist this
temptation.

At this point in the search process, board members often begin to identify their favorite candidates. Since this would be based on incomplete information, it would be wise to resist this temptation. The visits and the references will add substantial, important information for the board to consider. Reserving judgment until all the information is available assures that decisions are based on a great deal of data. In a best-case scenario the finalists will all continue to be exciting and interested. At times, however, the more comprehensive references or the meetings with the community reveal concerns that were not visible in the initial interview. Or, one or more candidates will appear even stronger than the first impressions indicated. The visits and the references will add greatly to the work completed to this point. Keeping an open mind leaves room for incorporating valuable new information.

Communication with the community

The chair of the search committee can prepare the community for this next phase personally and in writing. An overview of the process, the "bios," information about how the finalists were chosen and their experience relevant to the nonprofit's goals, will bring everyone up to date. Ideally, it is preferable to meet directly with constituent groups to explain the purpose of these visits. People can then ask questions, with the result that constituents will be clear about the process and the goals.

Staff and board members need to be aware that they are now participating in the recruitment of the next executive director as well as forming impressions about the fit. Candidates also want to learn much more about the organization, since they are considering a major career move and will want to ask questions as well as answer them.

Therefore, the search committee and the board have to "set the stage" for these visits, explaining to the community the dual purpose of the meetings about to take place. The constituents know that a search was under way and is proceeding on target, but this is their first look at the results. Naturally, they are curious and want to evaluate what the committee has done. While that is understandable, the community has to temper its evaluative mode with courtesy and hospitality for its guests, just as the search committee did.

A positive, forward-looking message from the chair of the search committee or the board, or both, can set the tone in preparing those who will meet candidates. Part of the explanation is that just as the organization has choices, the candidates do also. The community has the opportunity to share the best attributes of the organization as well as goals or challenges for the future, and in the process to help recruit the next executive director as well as learn about each finalist's abilities and leadership style.

This is an important career decision for the finalists and probably also a personal and family decision which each candidate will be weighing carefully. Good leaders are not frightened by challenges, but they need to hear the positive aspects of the role as well. It can make a very negative impression if the

Staff and board members need to be aware that they are now participating in the recruitment of the next executive director as well as forming impressions about the fit.

candidates hear about nothing but the organization's past problems. Complaints, without the balance of assets or strengths, may jeopardize the opportunity to hire the person the board wants to select.

This is an opportunity to state the decision process again, a reminder that the board will incorporate all of the information in reaching its decision. That information includes interviews, other meetings, references and "impressions" (described later in this chapter) as finalists spend time in the community. The message needs to convey clearly that the board will make the decision based on all of the available information, including constituents' "impressions," which are one part of the total picture.

Information for finalists

Before the finalists arrive they will want additional materials from the organization and sufficient time to study them. Again, this information would be sent to the finalists at their home addresses. Here is a sample list:

Finance, fund-raising, program

- Financial statements,
- Feasibility study (or fund-raising documents),
- Long-range planning information (the last one or preliminary work on this one),
- Any accreditation report or funder's evaluation,
- Program descriptions.

Board

- Bylaws,
- Terms and term limits,
- Leadership development and/or succession plan,
- Regularly scheduled meetings,
- Committees and meeting times,
- Makeup of committees (board and staff),
- Brief description of board members (profiles).

Administration and staff

- List of administrators and profiles or "bios," if available, or a brief introduction,
- List of staff and data about education, credentialing, length of employment,
- Salary scale and benefits information,
- Employee handbook, if available, or personnel policies.

Area information

- Chamber of Commerce materials, including cultural and recreational attractions, colleges and universities,
- Housing or real estate information.

The schedule for the visit

- Meetings, times and places,
- The names and titles or roles of those individuals and groups attending. (Large groups can introduce themselves at the beginning of the meeting).
- Plans/schedule for the spouse, partner or family.

Candidates who are truly interested will read the information and demonstrate this through their questions or responses. If someone has not bothered to read the materials, this may imply either a lack of thoroughness or lack of interest.

If someone has not bothered to read the materials, this may imply either a lack of thoroughness or lack of interest.

Including family members

When a candidate is considering a move from a different state, he or she also has a more complicated personal decision which may involve family. Typically, a nonprofit would invite the spouses or partners of the finalists to visit, because they will be a major part of the finalists' decisions. If another person is coming to visit, the organization should include him or her in the planning and find out ahead of time what he or she would like to do. This part of the plan might include a tour of the organization's facilities; other possibilities might be to see more of the city or area, explore housing or schools, or meet with people who work in the same field. When it is a couple or a family making the decision, this extra hospitality is an important and necessary part of the process.

When it is a couple or a family making the decision, this extra hospitality is an important and necessary part of the process.

As one of my former clients noted from his experience: "You ignore this at your peril!" The entire period of the finalists' visits combines evaluating as well as marketing by the organization to present its best features. At the same time, the finalists and their families are also carefully evaluating this career and personal move. Reluctant spouses or partners have changed their minds after a good experience. On the other hand, finalists have withdrawn if family members continue to object to the move.

The schedule

The finalists' impressions of the organization can also be shaped by welcoming people and a candidate-friendly schedule. Seven meetings a day, each time with a new group, is a test of fortitude. Having a larger number of meetings becomes counter-productive because community participants feel rushed and candidates are not satisfied with the results either. While the staff of the nonprofit will have many questions, the reality is that there will probably not be time to have all of them answered during the scheduled visits. The community will have a way to share their questions through the "impressions" discussed later in this chapter.

A totally rushed schedule is inconsiderate, does not reflect well on the organization and leaves everyone unsatisfied.

One nonprofit created an over-scheduled visit without enough time for finalists to get from one meeting to the next and too many meetings overall. Finalists and the constituent groups were frustrated because there was not enough time to develop real conversations. There were also no breaks in the planned schedule; during the first day one candidate had to demand a restroom break — not a great first impression. A totally rushed schedule is inconsiderate, does not reflect well on the organization and leaves everyone unsatisfied. Good planning and communication by the search committee and the board is key to successful visits and the learning they can provide.

Visits should be arranged so that finalists do not meet each other, just as in the case of search committee interviews.

To ease the visitors' days, it is helpful if members of the search committee or board serve as guides, announce the end of each meeting and direct the candidate to the next one so that each group has the allotted time. Visits should be arranged so that finalists do not meet each other, just as in the case of search committee interviews. That situation would be awkward and embarrassing for the candidates and would not provide the focus the board and community need to concentrate on one finalist at a time.

With a welcoming and candidate-friendly schedule for the finalist, the organization also needs to be considerate of the interests and questions which family members have. The person who is coordinating the schedule with the finalist can inquire about what family members want to see during the visit and develop a schedule from those discussions. The "scheduler" can check in with the family members also and anticipate having other welcoming or social events, particularly if there are no scheduled events for the candidate's family on a particular day. A tour of the facility is helpful, or simply scheduling a luncheon. Family concerns are equally important; their feelings about the organization, the community and the geographic area are often a deciding factor in finalists' decision.

The number of days for each visit will depend on the size of the organization. Although more than one day may seem burdensome to the organization at first, the demands on most individuals will be minimal because each finalist will be meeting with different groups. Most of the search work has been successfully completed; this is a big decision and the extra days could make a difference. The search committee or board could also find additional volunteers to assist during the visits.

Sample schedule for the finalists

8-10 am	Breakfast meeting with the board
	Break
10:30	Tour facility and have a discussion with executive director, senior administrator, board or search committee member
11:30	Meet with senior administrators
12:30-1:30	Lunch with one or two people, search committee and/or board chair, executive director or a search committee member
	Break
2:00	Meeting with staff
	Break
3:30	Compensation and contract discussion
4:30	Wrap-up meeting

This sample, or something like it, would work for most small nonprofits. Larger ones would extend the visit to a second day. This schedule follows the seven-meetings-a-day advice; if more meetings are needed, the organization should plan a second day, or a portion of one, to avoid having people feel rushed.

The board could also have an evening meeting, if that would assure full attendance. An evening meeting before a full day schedule provides a more leisurely board event. There could be a formal board interview and discussion, followed by dinner with the finalist and his or her family.

A balance of questions and answers from the candidate and from the "audience" allows each to gather the needed information.

A combination of more informal, small meetings and larger groups is ideal. A balance of questions and answers from the candidate and from the "audience" allows each to gather the needed information. The goal of the meetings is to have conversations, not quizzes.

Usually finalists will meet the board, the current executive director, other senior administrators, staff and other constituencies which seem appropriate. Additional meetings might include clients and major donors or people from other funding sources. It may take some creativity to pare down the meetings for a reasonable visit. While it is often tempting to fill the days, the finalists also need time to catch their breath and be able to process what they are experiencing. Scheduling free time in a visit of several days would allow the finalists to see something they are interested in or simply have some time to rest and reflect.

It is difficult for an organization which is participatory in nature to fit everyone in, but it is important to figure out how to do that without exhausting the candidates and diminishing opportunities for real dialogue and learning. Trying to work out an acceptable schedule may convince the planners that a second day is necessary. Candidates may ask to meet specific people, which is also a factor in planning the schedule. Communication to the community can mention this scheduling dilemma and explain that the solution is the best the committee could create.

Impressions

A nonprofit organization will want to provide a way for people who meet the finalists to offer their impressions. For a small organization, this might be in discussions. For a larger organization, one possibility is the following impressions form, which can be adapted to fit an organization's needs. In explaining the form, or in discussions about it, the message needs to be clear that this is an individual's impression, most likely gathered in the space of an hour. The board will be reaching a decision based on a comprehensive package of information, including many long conversations and extensive reference checks. The form is designed so that it is clear that the board is seeking impressions but that this is not a voting exercise. Question three offers a way for people to voice concerns, and gives the board the responsibility of finding answers.

Sample impressions form

Name of organization:

Name of finalist:

1. What valuable experience would this candidate bring to the organization?

2. What is your sense of the candidate's leadership style and its fit here?

3. What questions would you like the board to ask references?

4. Other comments.

Your name (optional):

Your role:

Return this form to:

Maximizing the visits

Prior to these visits, the search committee chair should have had a telephone discussion with candidates to assure that the finalists' salaries are not beyond what the organization can afford to pay. During the visits, the board chair can further discuss salary to be sure there are no unanticipated obstacles with the compensation package or with the proposed contract. Because a finalist's acceptance of the position may hinge on the specific contract, having a draft available for discussion is helpful. These discussions do not constitute an offer but are raising important issues in order to clarify them now. This preparation reduces the time a finalist would need before accepting the board's offer. Chapter Seven discusses the contents of contracts and Chapter Twenty explains how this initial preparation can ease the selection process.

Debriefing each finalist at the end of his or her visit allows the search committee to learn more about how observant each person is, what his or her concerns may be and the level of his or her interest.

Debriefing each finalist at the end of his or her visit allows the search committee to learn more about how observant each person is, what his or her concerns may be and the level of his or her interest. The candidate has the opportunity to share his or her impressions and to ask any additional questions. This is the time when the board needs to ask and to know if the candidate would take the position if the board offers it. If there are any outstanding issues, the board would also want to know those at this point to determine if they are major or negotiable. This preparation will provide up-to-date and useful information as the board compiles information in order to choose the next executive director. These steps will increase the chances that when the board chooses, the finalist of its choice will be ready to accept.

Further reflections or family dynamics could bring up new issues after the finalists' visits. The board chair can invite each finalist to call with any subsequent thoughts or questions.

Planning references and workplace visits

References, which would begin while the visits are in the planning stage, are discussed in depth in the next chapter. Also in that chapter is information on requesting additional data. Since references and the requests take several weeks, they need to be part of the plan at this point. The goal is to have all of the information the board needs to make its decision by the time the finalists' visits conclude. Most likely the finalists' visits are several weeks away while the organization prepares. During this time, the references can be a priority.

It may be possible for a small number of search committee or board members to visit the finalists in their current workplace and have face-to-face meetings with references. The value of these meetings is that search committee or board members will get a better sense of the organizations, their cultures, the environments and the finalists' influence. The candidate can help to plan these visits, which should be as unobtrusive as he or she wishes, while adding to the knowledge base. If workplace visits are planned, the board chair should call his or her counterpart and request permission to visit. If the finalist is not yet an executive director, the board chair should also call the executive director.

_____

This chapter has reviewed the necessary steps for planning the visits of finalists. While those visits are in the planning stage, comprehensive references are underway, the topic of the next chapter.

References and Other Necessary Data

This chapter explains how to check references thoroughly and effectively and how to find other data so that the board has comprehensive information before making its decision.

Introduction

Well-done references will round out the process as the search committee or board hears directly from people who work with the candidates.

At this point in the process, the finalists' visits are scheduled and the suspense is mounting as the time for a decision nears. A great deal of work has been done and a great deal of information has been gathered. Well-done references will round out the process as the search committee or board hears directly from people who work with the candidates. Each organization can determine whether the references will be conducted by the board chair, board members on the search committee or the search committee chair. Reading this chapter will prepare the callers for this important task.

References are a good way to gather substantial information from people who have observed a finalist in many situations. Hearing from references may confirm the impression of the candidate the search committee had after the first interview or it may raise questions. Just as a résumé writer may be modest or just the opposite, an interview can leave an impression of "nice person but can he/she do the job?" or, conversely, of someone who is the ideal candidate. Either impression is valid as long as everyone remembers that it is only an impression, a starting point for discovering more.

Thorough references can answer the obvious questions and the ones which will develop during conversations. There is a wealth of information available from people who have worked with a candidate and know him or her well. Hearing from them will give a search committee views of the individual from many perspectives — in both ordinary and challenging situations.

Calling people who know a candidate from different perspectives will illustrate how a person hires, mentors, supervises and supports.

Calling people who know a candidate from different perspectives will illustrate how a person hires, mentors, supervises and supports. Learning about the current employer — size and scope, challenges, successes and failures — will explain the complex situations the finalist has experienced and how the present work situation compares to that of the hiring organization.

Speaking with people at all levels of a candidate's current organization gives a well-rounded view. Hearing from people who report to the candidate, his or her peers and the person he or she reports to, will create a comprehensive overview. In any reference interview, understanding the reporting relationship, and the length of it, will help the caller tailor the questions to fit. A new employee will have one perspective on leadership style and mentoring while a seasoned employee has a different view and can provide a perspective of the candidate's development over time. A board member will have one view of a major challenge while a staff member may have another.

Whether or not to contact references at previous places of employment depends on several factors. The first is how long the finalist has been with his or her current organization and whether or not it would be relevant to call. References at a prior organization could shed light on the candidate's growth and development, which helps to understand him or her more fully.

Confidentiality and the timing of references

Candidates who need confidentiality will not want a lot of people to know about their application at the start of the search. The beginning period of the search process is exploratory as the committee and the candidate are figuring out whether there is mutual interest. At the point when there is some early interest the search committee could request preliminary references, a small number of people whom the candidate has told or is comfortable telling. That point is most likely after the telephone interview. No other references should be called until the candidate gives that specific permission.

It is critical that search committees remember that an individual's career is at stake and confidentiality has to be maintained until the finalist stage. If a potential candidate is tentatively exploring a possible move, he or she may not want to alarm anyone in the current workplace because any move to another position is far from certain. A candidate's board, supervisors and employees can become angry if they are informed too soon or accidentally. It also can be a problem for morale, hiring and possibly

It is critical that search committees remember that an individual's career is at stake and confidentiality has to be maintained until the finalist stage.

fund-raising at the candidate's current workplace.

An information leak could seriously damage a candidate's employment; if he or she is let go this could have a negative impact on future career opportunities. It is hard to predict an employer's response. In one case, an executive director, after seven years with an organization, informed his board chair that he was thinking about a change in the next couple of years. The board chair dismissed him immediately! This sudden departure was not good for the executive director or for the nonprofit. He actually fared better than the organization did.

While the example above is a worst-case scenario, it illustrates what can happen if an announcement is made prematurely. Certainly a search committee would not want a candidate to lose his or her job because word got out prematurely. Confidentiality is a responsibility that search committee members must be honor bound to take seriously. Frequent reminders are critical throughout the search process.

When a candidate is seriously interested in a new leadership role and has indications that the organization is also seriously interested, he or she would inform a board chair, perhaps the whole board and usually a few key colleagues. When the candidate is invited to become a finalist, the candidacy becomes very public. The person has determined that the job is interesting enough to warrant taking this step. And, at the finalist stage, the searching organization needs the freedom to make comprehensive reference calls.

The names of other candidates, who applied or were interested, always remain confidential.

The names of finalists are public after each person agrees to this. The names of other candidates, who applied or were interested, always remain confidential. This is not a place for compromise.

Preliminary references

The objective of the telephone interviews and preliminary references is to use the search committee's time most efficiently and effectively. At the leadership level, a nonprofit is often seeking candidates nationally, so interviews can also involve significant costs. Telephone interviews and preliminary references can provide more information as the search committee decides which candidates to interview. The candidate can provide a few names of references he or she trusts or has already told about the job, or someone who has left the agency or works for a former employer.

With good preparation, even preliminary references can be revealing. The tools provided in this chapter will help a search committee conduct informative preliminary reference interviews. This can confirm what has been learned through the telephone interviews or raise issues which make the search committee hesitant to proceed at all or without having additional information from the candidate or the perspectives of other references. Preliminary references become part of a candidate's overall file.

Comprehensive references

Respecting someone's need for confidentiality at the beginning of a search process is appropriate. When someone is a finalist and an organization is preparing to select its next leader, the situation is completely different. Now, the nonprofit has the obligation to conduct thorough and extensive references before making its hiring decision. By this time, the finalist has agreed to publicly visit the hiring organization and agreed to have references called.

Comprehensive references begin when a search committee has completed its interview process and recommended finalists to the board. By this time, a committee will have (or ask for) a list of additional references from each candidate. They may, or may not, have or want written references. While the written pieces may be informative, they are usually seen by the candidate, which limits how candid the writer is. Written references can gloss over important issues, may not answer the questions a committee wants to ask and are not interactive conversations which usually provide better data.

In addition to the list of references, a committee will want the permission of each finalist to talk with anyone who knows her or his professional work. It makes sense to have candidates sign a simple letter stating that they agree that this is acceptable.

The goal of reference checking is a comprehensive view of each finalist from every perspective. To accomplish this, those called as references should include:

- people for whom the candidate works or worked,
- peers, and
- people who work or worked for the candidate.

Work-related references provide solid data. People who are members of the same association are probably not useful unless the candidate had a real

Written references can gloss over important issues, may not answer the questions a committee wants to ask and are not interactive conversations which usually provide better data.

leadership role and can point to significant accomplishments. Professors can comment on academic ability, which is useful when that is relevant to the job. Personal references can provide a sense of someone's character and a means of knowing him or her in a different way, but they do not add to an understanding of someone in the workplace.

The search committee chair or board members will want to be rigorous in pursuing additional references that were not on the finalists' original lists.

The search committee chair or board members will want to be rigorous in pursuing additional references that were not on the finalists' original lists. This would only be done after the individuals have given permission to call potential references beyond their "official" list. To develop a list of people beyond the names provided, it is useful to picture an organizational chart; this will provide logical additions. Some of the additional references could include board members, the executive director or the chief financial officer, development director and program people. The organization's printed materials or Web site are useful sources of names, or simply calling the organization's business manager or development director would work. Other possible people to call are funders and clients.

In some cases, the "off the list" references will confirm what others had said about the candidate earlier; in other cases, they will provide completely new information. At times the additional information will be less complimentary than the earlier references, and at other times, the new references will be more glowing than the first ones. In any case, they are worth doing for the additional information they provide.

Going beyond the candidate's list of references assures a board of thoroughness and unbiased opinions. The first references will explain major challenges faced by a particular finalist and the next step would be to find people who may have been opposed to the outcome or adversely affected by the person's decision. They can be found by simply asking this reference, or a later one, for someone who was not happy with the outcome or the decision. It is important to remember that leaders have made difficult decisions and not everyone will be pleased. The way a candidate handled the process is important to understand, not the fact that there were some people who disagreed with the decision.

Planning before calling references

If the chairs of the board and search committee or other trustees will be calling references, they should begin with a planning session to assure that the work is coordinated and comprehensive. Answering the following questions will result in heightened awareness of what is involved in this process:

- What are the goals of the questions?
- What is the complete list of questions which fit our goals and needs?
- Who will make each call?
- What are the techniques for learning the most?
- How will callers report back to the committee or the board?
- How will follow-up or additional calls be coordinated?
- What is the deadline?

Deciding who will make the calls depends on the particular circumstances, the time constraints, the interest and the availability of callers. It might start with the search committee chair and the board chair and include others as needed.

A caller would review the candidate's résumé, the organization's goals and the list of questions to ask. The first step is to introduce oneself, the institution, the position for which the person is applying and then to ask if the person has fifteen or twenty minutes available at the moment. If not, one would make an appointment to talk later. In actuality a reference call may take longer than twenty minutes if the person is thoughtful, knowledgeable and interested in talking.

When the reference is ready, the caller would describe the position in terms of its challenges and its importance to the organization. Next he or she would begin the questions. Taking notes while listening and preparing to ask the next or follow-up question, requires some practice. Therefore, one idea is to start with an easy call, not the most important one. While it is possible to call someone back to check on something missed, it is preferable to complete the reference while the person is engaged the first time.

Open-ended questions provide the most information. An example might be: "Tell me about the organization and how you and the candidate work together?" A second question might be: "What are the major challenges?" Then, one could ask the candidate's role in working on a particularly difficult challenge. Another good question to ask is: "How have you seen this person grow and develop?" An easy follow-up question is: "What do you believe is the person's next learning curve?" This is a non-threatening way

Open-ended questions provide the most information.

of asking the reference to describe areas where the finalist is not as strong. Most likely this would not rule someone out at this stage but it would be useful information for the board in its decision-making process.

Well-done references help the board have an awareness of areas where the new executive director has a learning curve. The board can then work with the new leader to figure out a professional development strategy.

What a caller wants are specific examples/stories that illustrate what someone has done, why the candidate thought it was important and how they went about doing it – all of which provide a good perspective on leadership style and how someone analyzes a situation.

Throughout a conversation with a reference, the caller is creating opportunities for learning more about a particular candidate. Asking open-ended questions encourages the reference to explain, to share a story, to elaborate. The exact opposite of open-ended questions are those which only require a one-word answer. An example is: "Is this person a good worker?" A response of "yes" does not provide much information and a response of "no" would also need further explanation. Yes/no questions make it is easier to evade the truth because no details are required. What a caller wants are specific examples/stories that illustrate what someone has done, why the candidate thought it was important and how they went about doing it – all of which provide a good perspective on leadership style and how someone analyzes a situation.

General and specific information to gather

The ultimate objective is to develop new information and to verify or disprove the impressions gathered in the interviews. In their planning meeting, those who will be calling references can develop specific questions to compare a candidate's experience and abilities with the challenges the organization has. The following examples illustrate why each nonprofit can best create its own questions. If the hiring organization is fairly new and wants to develop to the next stage, questions can address experiences relevant to organizational growth and development. If the organization wants to evaluate and improve its programs, it will be looking for parallel experience. A small agency, which does great work but struggles for recognition and more stable or diversified funding, will have particular questions which fit its situation. Those who will call references can create a list of specific questions they want answered.

The following information is an overview of what to gather in each reference call:

- the reporting relationship of the reference and the candidate and how long they have worked together,
- the responsibilities of the candidate from this person's perspective,

- the challenges presented to the candidate,
- how he or she met those challenges,
- the state of the organization, program or department now,
- what might have worked better,
- what the candidate learned from challenges or over time/how he or she developed,
- other people who have a view of those challenges and the candidate's work.

Other ways to learn the most

Because the search committee and the board have agreed to confidentiality in all search matters including references, the caller can tell the person who is acting as a reference that what he or she says is confidential, that it will be shared with the board but not with others or with the candidate. This statement may encourage someone to be more candid. Having repeated this commitment to confidentiality, the caller will also be reminded of its importance.

Open-ended questions provide good information because most people like to talk about their work. When references have a chance to tell their story it helps the caller understand the context for the candidate's work, the kind of organization it is, the size comparison, the challenges and accomplishments. Stories provide background for the prepared questions and for those that develop during the conversation. When people are comfortable talking about their organization and the candidate, it is easier to ask difficult questions which were planned or for impromptu questions when new information appears.

People who work for nonprofit organizations feel connected to other similar agencies and often feel an obligation to be helpful — when the candidate is wonderful or not so wonderful. References in nonprofits are a completely different experience than in corporations where policies may limit conversations to dates of employment. The following example illustrates this.

In one search, the search committee was favorably impressed by a candidate whom they were considering as a finalist. As a next step, they began making reference calls. The first name on the list was a well-known person whose name regularly appeared in the news. The expectation was that this would be a positive reference because it was at the top of the list — but it was just the opposite. The almost immediate response of the reference was "I owe an

When references have a chance to tell their story it helps the caller understand the context for the candidate's work, the kind of organization it is, the size comparison, the challenges and accomplishments.

allegiance to our field and therefore I am going to tell you the truth about the person." It was not pretty. The short version is that the candidate was appropriately respectful to those to whom he reported, those in leadership positions, but consistently nasty to everyone else. It was not hard to get this information; the reference wanted to let people know.

It is important to realize that one negative reference could be the exception; it could be someone who disagreed with a decision the candidate made or simply a clash of personalities. In the case noted above, other references described the person's behavior in the same way. While the first name on a list of references rarely provides this level of candor, talking to enough people about a candidate will assure that the reference interviews are contributing to the development of a comprehensive picture. After each call it is useful to note where there is consistency, where there is inconsistency and what information is missing. This analysis can help to focus the next call.

An important skill in doing references is the ability to listen carefully and pay attention to long pauses or times when a reference seems hesitant.

An important skill in doing references is the ability to listen carefully and pay attention to long pauses or times when a reference seems hesitant. A reference who has been generally positive might be looking for an opening to reveal something else. At the end of the conversation, open-ended questions provide that opportunity. Examples are: "Is there anything else you would like to say?" "Do you have any hesitations?" "What haven't I asked you that you'd like to tell me?"

Knowing when the references are complete

A minimum of twelve to fifteen references for each candidate should assure a thorough understanding of the finalist from people he or she works for, peers and employees – including references not on the original list.

A minimum of twelve to fifteen references for each candidate should assure a thorough understanding of the finalist from people he or she works for, peers and employees – including references not on the original list. That thorough understanding means that all of the questions have been answered by several people and there is consistency. This number of references may seem like a lot of work, but they provide solid data that the board needs to make the best decision.

If there are conflicting views of a candidate, it may take longer to sort out and require doing additional references. It is possible that there will continue to be different perceptions. If the references are mixed, that is useful data, too, and the situation makes an interesting contrast with finalists whose references are more consistent. It is a judgment call to decide how far to go with someone whose references are inconsistent. While leaders routinely make difficult decisions which make some people unhappy, most people respect a leader whom they believe has listened, been fair in reaching a decision and open in explaining why the decision was made. If too many people have negative things to say about a finalist, that is obviously a danger sign.

Verification of credentials

References provide one kind of verification. A search committee can also check college degrees and required licensing information. A call to the college or licensing bureau first will assure that a letter, usually necessary, goes to the right department and that required information is included — they might require the person's date of birth or social security number. There might also be a small fee. A few colleges and universities require a signed letter from the candidate.

If time is a factor, the information can be faxed with written confirmation to follow. Explaining the reason for the request and providing a request on agency letterhead is usually sufficient. Verifying degrees and other credentials is easily done, and these are important, additional pieces of necessary data.

Background checks

Public agencies usually require background checks. Many private nonprofits want this additional assurance. The least expensive option for a nonprofit is a criminal, traffic and tax search. The Yellow Pages list agencies; many large, well known companies offer this simple computerized background check and will provide a report in two or three weeks. To assure the most useful information, a board would want to be very specific about the request. The organization's lawyer or a lawyer on the board can describe the extent of information to request and the exact wording of the request. A lawyer may also be able to recommend companies that do this work.

Following the guidelines about references and other data gathering will enable search committee or board members to gather comprehensive information to support the decision-making process. That process is the subject of the next chapter.

Selecting the New Leader

The information in this chapter will support boards as they work through the selection process using all of the information available from the interviews, references and visits. Included also are strategies for developing consensus and ideas for celebrating the decision.

Introduction

The selection of the next executive director is the culmination of a long and thorough process. The discussion and ultimate decision can reaffirm priorities and goals and develop consensus and excitement about the board's role and the organization's future. To prepare for the board meeting, each trustee has the following information to review:

- the goals,
- the required experience,
- the preferred experience,
- the finalists' materials,
- the search committee's report,
- the comprehensive references,
- his or her notes from the finalists' visits,
- an overview of the impressions forms,
- a report on visits to the finalists' organizations, if this was part of the process, and
- degree and credential verification.

The safest course is to plan for ample time to reach a decision and to have an offer accepted. The communication to the community about the selection process should take into account that extra time may be needed for negotiations or other unexpected delays. It is easier to make an announcement earlier than expected, rather than later, which can cause anxiety about the time a decision is taking.

The process

There is a great deal of information to be absorbed and analyzed. A board will want to be certain that its decision will have successful, long-lasting results. A thorough discussion of the information will assure that this important decision is a thoughtful one. Ideally the extent of the available information will be the basis for the decision and diminish a preference for a "favorite" based on less thorough analysis.

The board now has the benefit of the comprehensive references, of meeting candidates at length during their visits, and of hearing about the visits to the candidates' organizations if those were part of the process. It has the original description with the goals and the ideal experience and abilities of the next executive director. The search committee might have used a grid as a visual reminder of the required experience and the "preferred" areas. A board might find this useful or might decide to create its own version as a way of beginning the conversation. Grids or charts can be useful as long as they are used to begin the dialogue, not in place of it.

Good board dialogues will link a person's qualifications, skills, experience and other qualities with the stated goals. The goal of the discussion is to see which finalist is closest to the "ideal" as the board weighs and discusses each finalist in the light of what the organization hopes to accomplish. In reality, the finalists will have different mixes of experiences and abilities, all variations of the "ideal." The board's task is to sort out the best choice for the organization at this time.

A useful question to ask is which experience and abilities are critical to success in the position and which can be learned. The discussions should also take into account what staff or board support is available in areas where a candidate has a significant learning curve. Answering these questions will help to refine the options further.

Hearing from each trustee, in turn, assures that everyone participates and that the board benefits from the collective wisdom. Continually refining the options, adding more information, developing new insights and thoughtfully inching towards a decision is the way to assure that this important choice is the right one.

Ideally the extent of the available information will be the basis for the decision and diminish a preference for a "favorite" based on less thorough analysis.

Continually refining the options, adding more information, developing new insights and thoughtfully inching towards a decision is the way to assure that this important choice is the right one.

After each trustee has contributed his or her thoughts, a board could assess its comfort with continuing in this discussion mode. An alternative or addition would be to chart the data for each candidate; this might be more comfortable for some groups. The board would then have a visual tool and a way to record what is being said. This chart can be created in the meeting, with everyone contributing so that the dialogue continues. It could include strengths in the required experience areas, additional assets, strong and positive references, and an impressive showing during the finalists' discussions in the community.

Each board member should feel that the discussion has been thorough before a vote takes place. Ideally, the decision can be a unanimous one. While board members may have differences of opinion initially, thoughtful deliberations and respectful listening may bring a consensus. If appropriate, the chair can ask if the board is comfortable declaring the decision unanimous.

Quaker meetings offer a way to develop unanimity and assure that everyone feels heard. In a Quaker meeting, the clerk would summarize the "sense of the meeting." An individual who did not wholeheartedly agree could announce he or she would "stand aside," voicing his or her feelings but respecting the views of others or the "sense of the meeting." Some variation of this method might help each board member feel heard, making it easier for him or her to support the decision which the majority of board members favor. Obviously a unanimous vote sends a strong message to the new executive director and to all constituencies.

Obviously a unanimous vote sends a strong message to the new executive director and to all constituencies.

Confidentiality and contingency planning

There is another decision which the board can make. If the organization's first choice should decline, is the group comfortable with making an offer to another finalist? This is possible when the finalists are fairly equal in experience and strengths.

Often the decision is close and the board would be comfortable with another finalist if the first declines. If compensation and contract conversations took place during the finalists' visits, this speeds up the acceptance time so that a board could go to another candidate quickly if its initial offer is not accepted. The board should discuss and agree on how much time is reasonable before the person responds to an offer.

Confidentiality about the selection is again critical until the decision is made and the letter of intent, or contract, is signed. There is no reason for anyone beyond the board to ever know if a finalist declined. That information could cast an unnecessary cloud on what should be a celebration of the new leader. It may also raise unnecessary doubts about the process or the decision. In several instances where organizations have lost their first choice and selected the next person, the results have been so successful that board members later wondered why they had any hesitation at all or why this person was not their original choice. Wisely, the boards did not share information about what had occurred.

The commitment

Because the board prepared for this event during the visits of finalists, the response time should be minimal. Most of the issues, including compensation, will have been raised and discussed when the finalists made formal visits. Sample contracts were also reviewed at that time. All of this preparation will minimize the time needed for the person the board selects to make a decision.

Usually it is the chair of the board who calls the person selected. Ideally, he or she could accept immediately based on the prior discussions. Most likely he or she will want to see a final version of the contract, so the board should have it ready because the goal is to have an answer as soon as possible. If there are no major differences, a simple letter of intent can suffice until the final contract details are acceptable to each party.

Notifying other finalists, the staff, constituents, funders and supporters

Once the board's offer is accepted and there is a signed contract or letter of intent, the chair of the board can personally call the other finalists. Understandably some boards prefer to wait for the signed contract before making any announcement. The call to other finalists can be followed with a personal letter. By this time, the search committee will have notified all other candidates, since they were not invited to be finalists.

When a board is preparing an announcement to the community it helps to reinforce the wisdom of the choice by linking the organization's goals with the next executive director's experience. Other aspects of the decision process can be provided to share the excitement people feel. Examples are a unanimous decision by the board or a particularly striking comment from a reference or member of the community. Because of the commitment to confidentiality, the positive words of a reference would simply state: "Someone who works with our new executive director confirmed our observations by saying: "… ." Or the board chair could request permission to identify the reference directly. If the comment was provided by a community member, he or she would need to agree to being quoted directly.

Ideally the board chair can meet with staff to announce the decision. An alternative is to have the vice-chair of the board or the search committee chair meet with staff members. Another option or addition is to send staff a letter (distributed in office mail boxes or mailed to their homes) or e-mail. For constituents, some of the choices are an immediate letter, an announcement in the next newsletter, e-mails or a posting on the organization's Web site.

The way funders and other supporters will hear depends on the existing relationships. Personal calls may be preferable for some, while the board chair's letter or newsletter will probably be the way most people outside of the organization hear. If finalists met with any of these individuals, a personal call is better.

Resources are another group to notify; these are the people who were particularly helpful in identifying candidates or providing references. Like the announcements to constituent groups, this letter can link the hiring decision to the strategic goals.

Public relations

Major transitions are valuable opportunities for bringing positive attention to an organization.

Major transitions are valuable opportunities for bringing positive attention to an organization. The board should brainstorm all the possible places for announcements, including local newspapers, local and national association bulletins, journals, all of the organization's publications, the Web site and everyone on its mailing list. The search committee and staff can brainstorm other possibilities.

The announcement can highlight the leadership selection as well as the organization's other recent successes. Linking the hiring to the organization's goals is another way to tell more about future plans.

Another possibility to celebrate this important decision is to provide opportunities to meet the new executive director. There might be several receptions, some geared to internal purposes and others designed to introduce the newcomer to professionals at other nonprofits in the area or to funders, supporters or donors. This can also be a useful time for bridge building with other agencies or for repairing strained relationships. All of these steps can be part of a conscious strategy developed for the transition process.

This chapter has encouraged boards to be thoughtful in making this important decision and thorough in celebrating and communicating it. The following chapter introduces the next phase of transition planning to support the success of the new executive director and the organization.

Transition

The goal of this chapter is to build on the positive momentum of the search process by identifying effective strategies for implementing a smooth transition to new leadership.

Introduction

A successful search is cause for celebration. Through the process, the board and the search committee have become much more knowledgeable about the entire organization, appreciative of different perspectives and excited about the future. Despite all the unknowns at the beginning of the search, the anxious moments and the unexpected situations which always occur, the results have been successful; the board has approved the process and made an offer which was accepted.

The remaining work is to assure that the transition is as productive and successful as the search was.

People feel a sense of accomplishment and are relieved to have moved successfully through the many phases and decisions. Naturally, it feels as if the search is over, and it is time to accept congratulations and assume that the work is done. However the next phase, the process of transition, is just beginning. In order to arrive at this moment, many people contributed a lot of time, energy and wisdom; a thoughtful transition will balance all of those efforts. The remaining work is to assure that the transition is as productive and successful as the search was.

Understanding transitions through the experience of other organizations

Transitions which bring in new leaders are a neglected area which too often receive little attention. To understand that process more thoroughly I visited seven organizations, all former clients. The goal of the interviews was to learn more about what new leaders found, wished they had known or wished they had available to them. There was also an opportunity to see how these executive directors were faring at different stages of their tenures. Highlights from these interviews illustrate why attention to this transition is critical.

The interviews ranged from an executive director completing her first year to another completing his twelfth year. In some instances, search committee members or board chairs added their thoughts, although this was not possible at organizations where the executive director had served for ten and thirteen years, respectively. At one organization the interviews included the current executive director, a search committee co-chair and the co-founders/co-directors who had retired after thirty-three years. There were fourteen interviews in all, which provided useful insights, examples of thoughtful planning and evidence of circumstances when lack of transition planning made the new leader's entry more difficult.

There was an enormous variety in transition planning — everything from virtually none at all to a very complete plan developed and carried out by the retiring co-founders with the help of the board. Where there was little thought given to the transition, the executive directors had to develop their own ways of learning — at the same time that they were expected to be providing leadership.

Those individuals, who arrived without the benefit of any transition planning, consistently found their first year difficult and found themselves having to be more responsive than strategic. On occasion, the result of their immediate immersion in problems and details was that people in the organization were disappointed because they did not feel they were getting to know their new leader or that the person was interested in what they were doing.

The following sections describe a thoughtful transition plan. There are examples from the interviews of how planning helped to ease the transitions and where the lack of planning made the transitions more difficult.

The benefits of transition planning

Planning will make the first year more productive, less stressful, and more reflective of the community's best intentions. The most effective way to begin a transition plan is to establish a committee to work on it. Having a transition committee centers the planning and gives it focus. This committee can help to ease both the professional and personal transitions for the new executive director and his or her family. The new committee could be a continuation of the search committee or a new group with representatives from board, staff and other constituencies.

Having a transition committee centers the planning and gives it focus.

A new leader wants to know the people in the organization and, through them, understand program and resource issues. This takes focused time before he or she knows enough to begin making big decisions for the organization. At the same time, staff, board, funders and the community want to get to know this new executive director. Because first impressions are important, a well-planned transition recognizes the time needed for the important people phase. This sensitivity to a learning and "getting-to know-people" phase will also provide the time and perspective for the new leader to begin developing a list of priorities to share and compare with the board's perceptions of the needs. If daily demands shortcut the learning time, it is difficult to step back and create a big picture view and be able to prioritize thoughtfully.

Developing a plan

An effective transition plan would cover the following topics.

The out-going executive director

Because the out-going leader may still be in place, any plan has to be considerate of his or her feelings. Consultation, before the plan is formed, will help both sides clarify what they need.

Pre-visits

The transition committee can determine times when the new executive director could come to visit before his or her actual starting date. These visits accomplish dual objectives. The new leader can be available for organizational events or meetings with board and staff and, on the personal side, can work on a housing search. In planning these visits, the board and transition committee, in consultation with the current executive director, can determine which decisions should include the new person and which events he or she might like to see or are good occasions for the community to get to know the next leader.

Introduction to operational areas

A plan which outlines each area of orientation for the new leader, and the person who will lead the orientation for that phase, paves the way for a thoughtful transition. First are the obvious operational issues, including finances, fund-raising , program areas, facilities and any key deadlines. The guides could include the out-going executive director, board members and administrators.

Introduction to the culture and the people

If a new leader does not understand an organization's traditions or way of doing things, he or she can do or say something which alarms people, who may think that this person will never fit. That does not make a good first impression — and it can easily be avoided with a little thought ahead of time. The transition team should tell the new executive director about important traditions or time-honored ways of doing things. Most likely, the history, values, philosophy and "culture" were discussed during the search process, but the new executive director now needs a more comprehensive version. Providing this background is important so that the new leader becomes part of the community more easily and is not seen as "that outsider" because he or she did something which upset staff or constituents. Explaining who the key people are in a non-judgmental but informative way helps the new leader begin to understand the diverse personalities as well as people's history with the organization.

If a new leader does not understand an organization's traditions or way of doing things, he or she can do or say something which alarms people, who may think that this person will never fit.

Introduction to the external community

Just as every nonprofit has its unique personality or culture, every city or town does also. The transition committee has a dual responsibility — to explain the internal culture and the "who's who" of the organization and to do the same for other important institutions in the surrounding area. The new executive director may have a sense of the external environment and how it affects the organization but, at this point, will want a more detailed description and analysis. Receptions to introduce the new person to other leaders in the area provide a quick start to the sense of place for the new leader and positive public relations for the organization.

The professional transition

The fourteen interviews about transitions showed that a lack of planning left new executive directors responding to multiple issues in the first year without having the time to figure out which areas were most important. In several instances, for different reasons, the departing executive directors gave an overview in a day or less. They were gone by the time the new executive directors knew what questions to ask.

One board had never set annual goals with the executive director, had never had an evaluation process and did not understand why it needed to change now. Until it did, the new executive director was trying to please everyone by

One board had never set annual goals with the executive director, had never had an evaluation process and did not understand why it needed to change now.

responding to each board member's suggestions, a wearying endeavor. Ultimately, the board did set goals and priorities which helped the new leader focus energy and attention where the board agreed that it really mattered.

When a thoughtful orientation was not part of the transition planning, the executive directors were on their own to discover how the place worked, who and what was important and where the "minefields" were. The discovery process was demanding and time consuming. With a transition plan, the first weeks and months could have been spent more productively.

In several instances, critical financial or facilities issues needed more attention than either the new leader or the board expected. These issues absorbed time which would ideally have been spent getting to know people and programs in more depth. Everyone in the organization will want to know the new executive director when he or she arrives; the transition committee needs to assure there is time for that to happen.

One executive director spent a day or two a month at the new site over a period of several months, prior to actually beginning the job. These trips combined house-hunting with appearances and introductions at organizational events. Each time, he planned meetings with different staff. By the time he officially started, he and the organization were connected and ready to begin their work together. This was particularly useful because complicated land acquisition and neighborhood resistance issues required his immediate attention and leadership. Without those "pre-visits" he would not have had the time to get to know staff as well as he did by the time he officially arrived to begin work. This was the "ideal" transition plan, a good model.

The personal transition

Just as the new job is beginning, there are many personal, logistical issues to deal with simultaneously. If the new person is moving to another area, he or she has to find housing, health care providers, repair people and everything else it takes to settle in a new area. Helping a new executive director with some of the personal transition issues indicates a concern for the person and obviously helps someone acclimate more quickly and ease more comfortably into a new community and a new workplace.

A starting point is to provide resources for housing and some of the other transition issues mentioned above. One new executive director moved 1,500 miles, and no one thought to help her locate a place to live by showing her the area or suggesting realtors. She was totally on her own. In another instance, a transition committee supported a new leader by helping her locate realtors, and when she signed the purchase papers on a new home, people brought take-out food from neighborhood restaurants — a much warmer beginning.

Family members also have questions and needs and appreciate recognition. Explaining and, even better, taking the newcomers to cultural and recreational attractions acquaints them with a new area and is welcome hospitality. The transition committee can also plan individual or social events to fit the family's interests. The objective is to welcome the newcomers into the community immediately and for board members to remember to include them in social or recreational events throughout the year. When the family feels welcome and comfortable in its new community, the executive director has one less worry.

Dealing with surprises

Several leaders mentioned that a big surprise had been the complexity and attention needed in the area of facilities. One executive director discovered problems with recently purchased property where there were major political issues in developing it. Three other new executive directors were unaware of the extent of neighborhood resistance to new building projects and the political and financial hurdles to overcome. These problems changed the whole nature of their jobs for the first year, something neither they, nor the board, realized would happen.

The result was that the new leaders found the bulk of their time consumed with issues they had not foreseen. The executive director who followed the co-directors fared best because he had had multiple opportunities to connect with the staff and the board before discovering the size of the facilities issues. The other three leaders who discovered facilities problems felt they spent the first year responding to unforeseen crises, and only in their second year were they able to step back and prioritize.

For other new leaders, their introductory time was spent dealing with very costly deferred maintenance issues with no plan in the budget for beginning the work. One leader was dismayed by the dreary appearance of the facility and the realization that she seemed to be the only one who noticed. She did not act immediately but wisely waited to figure out how to help create an attitude shift.

A thoughtful transition plan would have taken into account the time that facilities development would take and either planned ahead, so the new leaders had more time before their official start date, or had board retreats to establish priorities, short-term and long-term, and how the board could be supportive. This would have provided some focus to the hectic beginnings and helped to distribute some of the facilities work. It would also have demonstrated to the boards how many different areas were vying for the new executive directors' attention.

Another new executive director had not realized how much time the board required in addition to the myriad of other priorities. That particular board had not identified how it needed to grow and develop after the retirement of the long-term executive director. This is one of the reasons that boards need to work on their own professional development before hiring a new leader.

The following comments highlight some of the transition issues which new leaders encountered:

- "In the first year, there simply was not enough time. They wanted me to decide everything.I needed to make connections with every constituency. The board felt it wasn't getting enough of my time."

- "Because there were so many unresolved issues that needed my attention, the staff felt I was uninterested in them."

- "There are many hard problems as the executive director and you have to pick the most productive ones to work on or your energy and attention get diffused."

- "I inherited tough personnel issues. They take it out of you the most and often consume the most psychic energy."

Planning would have made these transitions better.

Supporting the success of the new executive director

Once the organization has found the perfect person, it wants to support his or her success. Positive first impressions are important and will be hampered if an executive director is consumed with serious financial or organizational problems which make him or her seem unapproachable. This is unfortunate, particularly when it happens after a successful search when people were so enthusiastic about the board's selection. A poor first impression is hard to overcome later.

Thoughtful transition plans could have made the first year smoother in six of the seven organizations; the seventh went smoothly because of the planning. The goal of a transition plan is to be aware of organizational issues, and the time those will consume, so that the plan still holds sacred the "getting-to-know-people time." The fourteen interviews illustrated the sheer number of demands on new leaders and, therefore, the necessity of a plan which sets up priorities.

Ideally, there can be a way to do pre-visits before the actual starting date. Well-planned visits before the new executive director officially takes over will result in more time to know people and to develop a sense of priorities as a useful background for assuming leadership.

Most likely the new leader is stronger in some areas than others. The comprehensive references are valuable again and the new executive director may have candidly indicated areas where he or she wants to grow. Within the first year's plans should be a means for professional development.

Being an executive director can be an isolating job; having support from the board is critical. Those boards which proactively developed their abilities to guide and support the new leaders were prepared to be productive partners. Earlier in the book, in Chapters Two and Three, is the premise that a transition to a new leader is the perfect time to develop the board's effectiveness. Ideally some of this work has preceded the selection decision so the board is ready to support the work of its new executive director. If not, the board can identify outside resources so that it can develop new skills and insights quickly.

Being an executive director can be an isolating job; having support from the board is critical.

Setting priorities

If there are time-consuming and critical issues which will face the new executive director as soon as he or she officially begins, it is even more important to plan the transition thoughtfully. One way to allow time for the new leader to get to know the people in the organization is for the board and the transition committee to identify the areas which need immediate attention and determine how to manage them. This plan may result in the delay of some non-critical decisions or delegating an area to someone else, either in the administration or on the board, who can manage an area while the new executive director is getting acclimated.

Reassessing the plan

After the new executive director has met with staff, board and other constituents and had a chance to absorb, analyze and prioritize, he or she can
share this perspective with the board. The new leader and the board can
then see if their sense of priorities is the same and discuss and resolve any
differences in perception. The dialogue can move on to identifying board
responsibilities, those which are primarily the executive director's, and
areas that overlap. When there is general agreement, the goals and priorities can be included in the executive director's annual goals as well as
those of the board. This becomes a useful guide as well as a tool for checking on progress.

The board chair and the executive director

Any nonprofit will benefit from a strong partnership between the executive
director and the chair of the board. The board chair and the executive director can have informal discussions about their leadership styles and any
adjustments either needs to make to assure a smooth working relationship.
The board chair and the new executive director also need an initial dialogue
about which issues are important to discuss and how often they will talk or
meet. After a while, each might ask if communication is timely and sufficient, or even too much.

One new executive director wanted goals and an evaluation annually so
that she would have a sense of how the board viewed her job performance.
Being this specific was new for the organization and it took them almost a
year to accept that it would be useful. Ultimately, having the written
agreement on goals, the informal discussions on progress and then a formal year-end evaluation helped the executive director feel more in control
of her destiny, knowing precisely how the board thought she was doing. A
second benefit was the clear focus which the goal-setting provided.

Another executive director tended to feel that he should handle difficult
issues and not lean on the board chair. He also worried about stepping on
the chair's "turf." While their relationship was working, the organization
might have benefited from more discussion between them and another
vantage point on difficult issues. Dialogues between the executive director
and board chair could have differentiated between what was information-
al and where advice or a decision was sought; this would help each be

clear about "turf" issues. There could have been open discussions on whether either felt there was a boundary issue. An informal talk about the expectations each had of the other would have made them both more comfortable and able to speak candidly. The section on "Policies and Operations" in Chapter Three has useful examples for dealing with boundary issues.

Starting off well is always the best option. Developing good relationships and the confidence to evaluate what is needed as the relationship develops is important for the boards, the executive directors and the organizations.

Developing reasonable goals

Each leader, in addition to transitioning into a new organization — and often into a new community, city or town — will be given a long list of board goals and, at the same time, will have goals he or she identifies through meetings with staff and constituents. Dialogues between the board and the new executive director serve to develop consensus on priorities, take into account new developments, and develop strategies for adapting when necessary. Time lines have to be amended when the unexpected happens. The board can help guide the executive director during the first year by having a dialogue about priorities and goals and re-examining them each month. The results will be to:

- guide re-prioritizing in the light of new information,
- assure that everyone understands the expectations, and
- re-articulate long-term goals while narrowing the annual goals to those that can be reasonably accomplished.

Planning will help to make the transition a positive one, even when unexpected issues consume major time. A dialogue about priorities will help a board and its new leader find ways to deal with the most important issues while also recognizing the need for working on the transition so that those first important impressions are positive ones.

A transition plan is considerate of the new leader and helps assure that important goals get the attention they need. Unexpected events often occur during the first year, as the board and its new executive director are beginning to develop their relationship. Thorough planning provides a foundation for relationships and dialogues so that any problems are taken in stride.

Keeping your executive director

Obviously boards want successful executive directors to stay. Some of the
ways to help that are:

- having an effective and supportive board,

- using goal setting as a basis for a constructive evaluation for the
  executive director,

- doing the same for the board,

- appropriately recognizing and showing appreciation for the executive
  director's accomplishments,

- supporting a director's desire for professional development and/or a
  leadership role in professional organizations, and

- providing compensation and benefits which considers the experience
  of the executive director and is comparable to that of others.

This is a the beginning of a list which each board can expand.

---

*The successful conclusion of a search
often leaves people feeling euphoric. The
goal of this final chapter is to encourage
a thoughtful transition which uses this
positive energy to support the success of
the new executive director.*

Appendices

Appendix A: Checklist / Reminders

Planning and Preparation

1. Develop a vision for the future and organizational goals. (Chapters One and Four)

2. Make maximum use of the potential inherent in the search process. (Chapters One through Four)

3. Work proactively to overcome constituents' anxiety. (Chapters Two and Four)

4. Assess and develop the board's readiness to lead the transition. (Chapter Two)

5. Develop a comprehensive plan for the search. (Chapter Four).

6. Assess the need for an interim director and the pros and cons of the decision. (Chapter Four)

7. Evaluate the need for professional assistance. (Chapter Four and Appendix C)

8. Develop the board's ability to attract great candidates and to work productively with its new executive director. (Chapter Three)

The Search Committee

9. Discuss and make very clear the responsibility and authority of the search committee. (Chapter Two)

10. Understand the legal and ethical obligations and how they impact each phase of the process. (Chapter Seven)

11. While selecting committee members, the board develops and explains the search time line and the process to reduce the community's anxiety. (Chapter Four)

12. Communicate regularly with the community during the search process. (Chapter Eight)

13. Select a search committee chair and committee members carefully to achieve representation and bring together thoughtful people open to new learning and the perspectives of others. (Chapter Five)

14. Discuss ways to make the search committee most effective as a basis for planning the work. (Chapter Six)

15. Emphasize inclusion and broad outreach through policies and board leadership. (Chapter Four)

16. Understand how leadership needs change as an organization develops. (Chapter Nine)

17. Become familiar with the attributes of leadership to support the thorough evaluation of candidates. (Chapter Ten)

Developing the criteria statement

18. Think about marketing, describing the best features of the organization. (Chapter Eleven)

19. Describe challenges and goals. (Chapter Eleven)

20. Use required and preferred categories of experience knowledgeably in formulating the criteria for the next executive director. (Chapters Seven and Eleven)

21. Minimum requirements will ease the process of evaluating applications. (Chapter Seven)

Outreach

22. Plan the outreach strategically at the beginning of the search and assure that word will reach a broad and diverse audience. (Chapters Twelve and Thirteen)

23. Use active networking to broaden and deepen the pool of candidates. (Chapter Thirteen)

24. Check on progress weekly to determine the number of truly qualified and truly interested candidates. Continue "networking" until there is certainty about a strong group of candidates. (Chapter Thirteen)

Evaluating Applications

25. Acknowledge applications promptly and determine when other updates are required. (Chapter Fourteen)

26. Before reading résumés, review the criteria which the search committee established. (Chapter Fourteen)

27. Before setting up search committee interviews, conduct telephone interviews and preliminary reference interviews to be certain of a candidate's interest and to gain a more thorough sense of his or her work history and the possible "fit". (Chapters Fifteen and Nineteen)

Search Committee Interviews

28. Understand the ethical and legal guidelines which apply. (Chapter Seven)

29. Prepare interview questions which advance the committee's understanding of each person interviewed; ask all candidates the same questions. (Chapter Fifteen)

30. Frame interview questions to learn about leadership and management skills. (Chapter Sixteen)

31. After each interview, debrief to share and summarize what the committee has learned. (Chapter Sixteen)

32. Plan the process for selecting finalists. (Chapter Seventeen)

References and Credentials

33. Learn how to engage references to support thorough information gathering. (Chapter Nineteen)

34. Conduct a wide range of references to assure a comprehensive view and an in-depth understanding of each finalist. (Chapter Nineteen)

35. Have the finalists' lists of references and their permission to speak with others; be diligent about making additional reference calls. (Chapter Nineteen)

36. Verify credentials and discuss if background checks are necessary. (Chapter Nineteen)

The Finalists' Visits

37. Prepare the constituencies for meeting the finalists. (Chapter Eighteen)

38. Send finalists additional information. (Chapter Eighteen)

39. Remind constituencies of the decision-making process. (Chapter Eighteen)

40. Create a candidate-friendly schedule. (Chapter Eighteen)

41. Before finalists leave, be sure their questions and concerns are known and discussed. (Chapter Eighteen)

42. Design a thorough information-gathering and decision-making process before the board gathers to make its choice. (Chapter Twenty)

The Board's Decision-making Process

43. Prepare ahead so the chosen candidate can respond quickly. (Chapter Twenty)

44. Determine a course of action if the first choice declines. (Chapter Twenty)

45. Notify finalists who are not selected in a timely and considerate way. (Chapter Twenty)

46. Inform the search committee and staff as soon as possible. (Chapter Twenty)

Transition

47. Develop a public relations strategy to maximize this opportunity. (Chapter Twenty)

48. Prepare a transition plan to complete the work successfully. (Chapter Twenty one)

49. Evaluate and support the new executive director's professional and personal needs. (Chapter Twenty one)

50. Develop candor in executive director/board chair conversations so that each knows the other's style and expectations. (Chapter Twenty one)

51. Discuss, agree upon, and plan to re-visit annual goals each month.

Appendix B: An Interim Leader

This following material is a discussion of when an organization might consider hiring an interim director, the pros and cons of that decision, and advice on the selection process for an interim leader.

Introduction

Selecting an interim executive director may be necessary when the head of the organization leaves suddenly or gives short notice and the organization needs leadership during the search process. Hiring an interim leader is preferable to making a hasty decision about a permanent executive director. While the board may be anxious to do something quickly, it needs to remember the importance of the decision, the opportunities a good decision can bring, and the long-term potential of the organization which could be realized with the right executive director. An interim director is not necessary if the current executive director is not leaving immediately or if there are no major organizational problems which require change-agent solutions.

The potential benefits of hiring an interim leader

Hiring a respected interim executive director reduces the time pressure on the search process. When the board finds a very experienced person, he or she can bring a great deal of wisdom and experience, begin work quickly and focus on the important issues. This person will know how other organizations work and bring a useful perspective while figuring out how to adapt ideas to this setting. A good interim leader can assess the administrative structure and suggest other possibilities, and he or she can mentor and support key staff. Tension is greatly reduced and morale goes up when a competent person assumes a leadership role. Another benefit is that there will be less anxiety about the time a search will take.

The interim option may be a good choice when there are serious internal problems. An interim executive director can be working on problems which are hampering the organization at the present time and that problem-solving work will make the position more attractive to potential candidates. Because an interim executive director has a limited tenure and is most likely an experienced administrator, he or she can take care of problems before a new executive director arrives, easing that transition.

An experienced administrator, perhaps a retired executive director, can serve as a consultant to the board and staff, furthering the work of the organization, not just maintaining it. With an experienced person as a leader and advisor, a board may develop in the ways it has wanted to; this will allow the board to be better prepared to attract and evaluate candidates for the permanent position.

The drawbacks

Having an interim may mean a longer period of time between permanent executive directors while a thorough search is underway. This length of time may initially be uncomfortable for the organization, especially if a capital campaign is in the planning stages. It may also be a concern to funders when they first hear about it. Staff and constituents will worry about another change in leadership. Explaining why a board believes that an interim leader is the best alternative should ease concerns. Hiring an experienced person would also help.

The importance of the decision

Selecting an interim leader is a major decision and an early and visible one. It can have a positive effect on the success of the search for the permanent leader, in part because he or she can begin to solve existing problems. A thoughtful evaluation of the organization's needs and the individual candidates for the interim role will result in a decision which gives people confidence in the board's leadership and the search committee's early work.

Hiring an interim leader quickly may seem desirable, but that short-term solution can be costly if it does not work out and that situation would consume a great deal of the board's time counterproductively. There is more to be gained by establishing clear goals and evaluating candidates thoughtfully. A good decision can have a positive effect throughout the interim leader's tenure and illustrate the organization's ability to hire well. This will naturally reduce anxiety and signal to people that the next search will be done as wisely. Being thorough in this search will mean that the organization can not only function well, but can move forward during an interim's stay. Just as in the search for a permanent leader, the search committee benefits from seeing multiple candidates and conducting thorough references.

The unique circumstances of the nonprofit will determine if the search committee also conducts the search for the interim executive director, which is usually the case, or whether the board will be responsible. The board might take the leadership role if the search committee has not been formed or will not be ready for some time. It is also conceivable that the board will produce advertising and announcements to begin the outreach and then have the search committee pick up the process.

Internal vs. external interim director

There may be an internal person who has the capacity to fill in as an interim or acting director. The advantage is that this person knows the organization well and requires less learning time. An internal person may require more board mentoring and time, but the insider's development could be an asset for the organization. With support and clear goals, someone from within the organization can successfully provide the necessary leadership during the months a search will take.

However, if there are difficult issues to resolve, it may be awkward for an internal person to make unpopular decisions and then return to her or his former job. If it is a case of tough decisions, it might be better to hire an interim leader not affiliated with the organization. An outside person, who will serve for a specific period of time, can more easily shoulder the blame for unpopular but necessary decisions.

Potential candidates

While there are fewer people prepared, willing or available for an interim position, there are very able people who will be perfect for this short-term assignment. People who fill an interim role may have retired and find themselves missing work. Or, they may be people who are between jobs, perhaps because they have moved to a new area or because of down-sizing.

Retired executive directors who have served successfully in interim roles have shown an ability to analyze organizational issues quickly and figure out what needs to be done; they have also been a stabilizing and calming presence. Their work demonstrated a level of professionalism which people respected. At the end of their tenures, the results were noticeably stronger organizations and more knowledgeable boards.

Most of the time it is preferable that the interim leader is not a candidate for the permanent position and that this is made clear from the beginning. One reason is that when an interim leader is also a candidate he or she may not be comfortable making the difficult or unpopular decisions which the organization needs. Instead the interim spends time "running for office" and therefore does not want to make any decisions which may be unpopular. Since most interim executive directors are retired, this usually does not become an issue.

In a situation where the search committee wants the interim executive director to be a candidate, he or she would apply just as other candidates would, interview with the search committee and have references checked with former employers. It is important that the interim only become a declared candidate within the announced application period. Other candidates may ask if the interim person is applying and this may or may not discourage some people from submitting applications.

Supporting success

An interim search is more limited in the quantity of qualified candidates available, but the same thoughtfulness which accompanies a search for a long-term leader has to be part of this work. All of the steps that are important in hiring a permanent leader are important in hiring an interim leader. There would be the same emphasis on marketing the organization, clarifying goals, broad outreach, and good evaluation. The chapters on each of those topics will provide useful guidance. A well-reasoned, thorough and successful interim search can be a practice run for the permanent search. It also illustrates to constituents that the search and the organization are in good hands.

With guidance from the board, an interim leader can be very productive. The board's task is to develop very clear expectations. The goals for an interim executive director will be different from those of the permanent person because the interim most often will serve for a year or less. There will be some areas of simple organizational maintenance and some areas which need to continue moving forward. In cases where interim executive directors have been very experienced and very wise, he or she has been able to analyze situations, make the necessary decisions and help the organization move forward with its priorities and goals. The board can develop expectations linked to the number of immediate needs and the interim director's experience; the expectations can be amended or added to if there is positive progress.

One client summarized the important points in hiring and working with an interim from her "hard-won experience":

1. Select an experienced administrator.

2. Be clear from day one what the interim is expected to do.

3. Do not be too ambitious.

4. Make sure all constituencies (staff, clients, etc.) understand the limited role of the interim executive director.

Clear goals, drafted by the board and discussed with the interim leader, will provide agreement on the goals for the year or the period of time that the interim is expected to serve. Developing priorities is "an imperative," providing focus for the interim period. Having the goals in writing provides a guide and reminder. Informal discussions with the board chair, at least weekly, will help to keep the plan on track. Each month, a meeting of the board or executive committee can maintain the focus by being systematic about discussing each goal, its priority, progress and any problems.

Every meeting is also a reminder of the role and responsibilities of the board. This attention to priorities can have visible results in the board's development and its work.

The transition

Introducing a new interim director and acclimating him or her, if they are not familiar with the area, will ease the transition so that the person can focus on the organization and its needs. Someone who moves temporarily may need more personal support in terms of housing and learning about the particular community. Welcoming other family members and providing information they may need will ease their transition. The discomfort of a spouse who feels isolated in a new area will also affect the interim director. Some of the ideas in Chapter Twenty-one, The Transition, can ease the entry of an interim and his or her family. While the community may be new, the work of the organization will be familiar and that is where the interim needs to concentrate — with some transition help from the board, search committee or transition committee.

If a nonprofit selects an internal person, work on the transition is equally important. Because this person will return to his or her prior role, a board needs to pay attention to situations which might harm that person's image. The board can support the interim by being very clear about its goals, so the community understands the priorities and the tasks given to the interim director.

Selecting and supporting an interim director is a "practice run" for the search for a permanent executive director, with all the potential opportunities and possible problems.

Appendix C: Hiring a Consultant

The purpose of this section is to offer some criteria for judgments about whether or not to seek outside help with the search process, to provide information about the kinds of available services, and to offer advice if a nonprofit chooses to select and work with a consultant.

When it may not be necessary

Many nonprofits conduct searches successfully without using consultants. Some of the necessary ingredients are: a healthy, stable organization which is well-connected to other organizations, clarity about what the organization needs, and having someone, or a committee, who can dedicate time to the search. Another important asset is a good chair of the search committee and he or she will need administrative support.

Since advertisements are rarely the solution to a search, there has to be a commitment to active recruiting. Another key factor is the choice and preparation of the person, or people, who will be recruiting. Each recruiter needs to have enthusiasm about the organization and good judgment. He or she must be adept at marketing and good at evaluating.

It will also be helpful to have search committee members who have worked on other searches, but a first-time search committee might find the assistance it needs in these chapters. Ideally, an organization which has had difficulties in prior searches will find enough support in this book to proceed successfully. It would be useful to have the committee read and discuss the ideas presented in this book so that people have the same understanding of the process and the issues.

Assessing the needs

When there is doubt about the organization's ability to conduct the search on its own, the board can evaluate where a consultant could help. Making a list of the areas where the organization may need help will enable the board to decide how a consultant might assist. Here are some questions for the board to ask itself to help define its needs:

- What services do we want?
- Is it simply that we want to see more and stronger applications?
- Have we defined our criteria clearly?

- Are we good at marketing this opportunity?
- How many candidates do we want to see?
- Do we need help with references?
- Do we have organizational issues where a consultant could help?
- Are there sensitive issues where an outside, impartial person could be valuable?
- Can a consultant more easily speak with people in other organizations who know us?
- Has there been considerable leadership turnover that we do not fully understand?
- Are we replacing a founder or long-term executive director and need to assess what that means for the board, the search and the transition?
- Where else do we need help?

As a board discusses these questions it will better understand if it needs assistance, or how much or how little help is needed. An organization may feel it has the ability to conduct the search successfully but needs help with organizational issues such as board development or frequent leadership turnover. Consultants who specialize in nonprofit leadership and organizational development can help a board prepare for a successful search process. Associations or other nonprofit boards can recommend qualified people. Checking with a consultant's references will explain the quality of his or her work.

Types of search services available

Placement firms

These firms, or consultants, specialize in a specific field and gather the résumés of people interested in new jobs. Their service is placement of candidates, so usually the fee is less than that of a search firm which provides additional services described in the next section. In some fields, but usually at lower levels than that of executive director, placement firms work on contingency; contingency fees are paid only when a candidate is hired. A contingency arrangement for an executive director's position is not common and probably not desirable unless the search committee is also actively searching.

Search firms

For these firms, the client is the organization — not the job seekers. A search firm tailors a search to the needs of the organization and should invest time in calling a large number of sources and candidates to find the right ones for a specific organization. These firms offer other services as well — organizational analysis and support, assistance in developing goals and criteria, comprehensive evaluation of candidates and transition support. Most search firms work on a retainer which is paid in installments, and their fees are generally higher than placement firms because their services are more extensive. Most search firms will agree to complete a search to the client's satisfaction. Many also offer a one year guarantee, so that if the person selected does not work out for reasons which should have been foreseen, the firm would conduct another search for no additional professional fees.

Search "coaches"

Some consultants will "coach" a search committee at strategic points, teaching a committee to conduct a search as a professional would. This option works well for small nonprofits or organizations with limited finances who cannot afford to have a search consultant engaged in the whole search. The organization gains the expertise it needs at a much lower cost since most consultants would charge a daily rate. A "coach" could be hired to help develop the description of the strengths and challenges so that it is appealing to candidates, help create an outreach and networking plan, work with the committee to plan preliminary and committee interviews, explain how to do references well and support the transition planning once the new leader is selected. These meetings are spaced out over the course of the search process. Someone in a coaching role can also be a resource for questions and concerns which arise between meetings.

Comparing and Contrasting Services, Firms and Fees

The examples above illustrate some of the ways that consultants vary in approach and services. Reviewing written information from several firms, describing their services and client bases, will offer additional insights into the services and the differences. Seeing the materials from a number of consultants will help the search committee further refine its options and determine if a consultant is needed and which firm might be the most helpful. Knowing more about the specific services offered and former clients will aid a search committee or board in developing questions as they interview consultants. It is important to ask whether the person doing the presentation is the person who will be working on the search, how many searches he or she is doing currently and the qualifications of anyone else who will be working on any phase of the search.

References are important because the quality of the consultant's work will directly affect the quality of the search. The board would want to generate a list of questions in order to learn about a consultant's relationships with former clients and the results of the work. Some of the suggestions in Chapter Nineteen, "References," will be useful here. Important areas to investigate are: the relationship with prior clients, the availability or responsiveness of the consultant, the quality of candidates the consultant identified, the depth of information provided, and the long-term results. Thorough references will provide assurance that the board or search committee is choosing wisely.

Selecting a consultant is a mini-version of the next search. While "chemistry" or comfort is an initial response, it is not sufficient information for this important decision. Learning more from references now will validate the importance of this due diligence in hiring an executive director. The information gathered, expected or unexpected, will be a good learning experience, one of many to come.

Consulting fees

Consultants' costs will vary depending on the services offered, the size of the firm, the field and the geographic locale. Soliciting information from a variety of consultants will produce information specific to the search, the field and the area. There are at least three different ways that firms set fees:

- One is by percentage of the executive's first year's compensation, for example 33-1/3%.

- Another way is a flat fee not linked to compensation.

- A third possibility is to employ a consultant to work on an hourly or daily basis, particularly if an organization only wants help on specific tasks, the "coaching" model.

Most consultants will also charge separately for some related costs such as printing, mailings, advertising and travel. Before beginning a relationship with a consultant, a board would draft a detailed scope of services and a written agreement on terms, fees and related costs. A lawyer on the board or the organization's counsel can assist here. Or, the consultant may provide a contract which the organization can review and amend. The board and the search committee chair would agree ahead of time which meetings the consultant should attend and how often the consultant will be in touch with the search committee — this avoids misunderstandings later.

The questions at the beginning of the chapter will help to assess the needs of individual organizations. Those questions can also serve as a source of inquiries about a consultant's work with his or her former clients. A small nonprofit, or one which has had difficulties in the past, may increase its chances of success with some professional guidance. If an organization has a close relationship with a foundation, some funding may be available for organizational development or for a search for an executive director.

Working successfully with a consultant

If an organization hires a search consultant, the goal is to create a good working partnership with that person. Sharing sensitive information is key to the consultant's thorough understanding of the organization. A professional knows how to evaluate the information and how to use it.

Candidates may be more comfortable asking questions of a search consultant about sensitive issues which are not explicit in the written description. While the challenges and goals section of the description should convey the size of the tasks, it will probably not be in great detail. A consultant can explain the facts of a situation and the plans to remedy any problems. These conversations can offset rumors which do not always provide facts or the intended solutions. With or without a consultant, minimizing the organization's challenges could result in candidates who are not willing or able to accomplish what is needed.

A positive relationship with the chosen consultant can only enhance the outcome of the search. As a client, the search committee and board chairs would want to be available to answer questions and provide feedback. They would want to let the consultant know of events which affect the organization during the search. Good communication will assure that a search committee is using the consultant's expertise productively. Understanding the search process and the important issues would help a board have more knowledgeable dialogues with a consultant.

This section provided an introduction to questions of whether to use a consultant and, if the decision is to use outside help, information on how to select and work with a consultant.

Deadlines

Notes